Other works by Karl L. Dahlstrom are non-fiction and reflect the author's initial foray into writing:

The Organized Universe, Outskirts Press, 2013

The 2nd Reformation: A Concerned Christian's Critical Review of the Christian Church

THE
DNA
OF SCRIPTURE

How True Natural Science Confirms
the Holy Scriptures as True

KARL L. DAHLSTROM

WESTBOW·
PRESS
A DIVISION OF THOMAS NELSON
& ZONDERVAN

Bible Translations or Versions Reviewed and/or Utilized

KJV-King James Version
(AMPV) –Amplified Version
NAS -New American Standard Version
NIV -New International Version
NLT –New Living Testament
LBV -Living Bible Version
RSV -Revised Standard Version
PHI -New Testament in Modern English
WMS –The New Testament by Charles B. Williams
MOF –A New Translation of the Bible by James Moffatt

Scripture quotations not otherwise marked are from the Holy Bible, authorized King James Version, © 2006 by World Publishing Company, Nashville, TN.

WestBow Press books may be ordered through booksellers or by contacting:

WestBow Press
A Division of Thomas Nelson & Zondervan
1663 Liberty Drive
Bloomington, IN 47403
www.westbowpress.com
1 (866) 928-1240

ISBN: 978-1-4908-7600-9 (sc)
ISBN: 978-1-4908-7602-3 (hc)
ISBN: 978-1-4908-7601-6 (e)

Library of Congress Control Number: 2015905825

Print information available on the last page.

WestBow Press rev. date: 7/31/2015

CONTENTS

EPIGRAPH

"And it is easier for heaven and earth to pass, than one tittle of the law to fail."

Luke 16:17King James Version (KJV)

PREFACE

Among other reasons for writing my first two books, *The Organized Universe*, and The 2nd Reformation: A Concerned Christian's Critical Review of the Christian Church, and this book, I decided to take the advice of C. S. Lewis who urged Christians with a scientific aptitude to keep up with the science of their day because "[w]e have to answer the current scientific attitude towards Christianity, not the attitude which scientists adopted one hundred years ago." He also encouraged Christians to write books about science that would counter the materialist worldview implicitly by presenting "perfectly honest science". That challenge and encouragement hit the nail squarely on the head for that was exactly what I wanted to do. In my humble opinion, this was accomplished in *The Organized Universe* by using a relatively new and obscure natural law of science called Benford's Law of First Digits to disprove the godless Theory of Evolution as espoused by Charles Darwin and his subsequent modern day apologists. In the same vein, I am continuing that trend in this book, in the way of a sequel, by utilizing the same science in this case to prove the authenticity of the Bible as being the true Word of God as handed down in both the New and Old Testaments.

In effect, as Lewis states, always follow the argument wherever it might lead, without placing artificial barriers to the consideration of new ideas. The argument in this case has led to a paradigm shifting effect in the dismantling of Darwin's Theory of Evolution and a bridging of science and religion in demonstrating a scientific proof of the Bible.

In my ground breaking first book, *The Organized Universe*, we discussed how this obscure, natural law of science, known as Benford's Law of First

Digits, was able to prove that Darwin's Theory of Evolution—particularly its core postulate of Natural Selection—was flawed and has been a fraudulent claim by evolutionists for more than 150 years. Moreover, we were able to demonstrate, in considerable detail, that our thesis legally qualifies as a 'scientific critique' to evolution theory as now being taught in science classrooms across the nation and, as such, is eligible to be taught alongside it. We also revealed how anti-evolutionists, namely creation scientists and intelligent design advocates, have failed in their numerous legal attempts for inclusion in the science classroom and gave the reasons why.

In making the case that The Organized Universe (in textbook form) be used as a scientific critique of Darwinism in the science classroom, it was necessary not to invoke any religious theme or reference in keeping with the doctrine of separation of church and state as found in the First Amendment to the Constitution. Ever since the infamous Scopes Money Trial of 1925, the evolutionary battles have been waged in practically every state in the union mainly between creationists—wanting to have creation science or direct bible based teaching taught—and later, intelligent design advocates seeking an alternative forum to teach the observations of design in nature, thinly disguising their religious subtleties. All of their efforts to date have failed in their attempt to counter evolution in the schools.

Notwithstanding their efforts, we have managed to perform a quantum leap in attacking the problem of the de facto teaching of evolution in our schools without widespread challenge. We will seek to petition various state school boards to review and consider our work as a scientific critique of evolution thereby qualifying us under court decisions as an eligible participant in the science classroom. Should our petition efforts fail, we will then seek redress through the federal court system to uphold previous decisions regarding this issue. Our efforts will be ongoing in this pursuit and as such, we urge you to read The Organized Universe and get involved at the local level to combat the teaching of this theory in our educational system.

Consequently, with the publishing of *The Organized Universe* and the scientific proof of a universal order inherent in all matter and life forms, we set in motion a paradigm or idea shift in both scientific and conventional thought, particularly as to the *possibility* that some 'outside force', 'designer' or 'creator' set the universe in motion and provided that initial injection of life which has culminated in the abundance of life we have today. Evolutionists have never accounted for this initial force of life and, as Darwin did, simply ignored the question of the origin of life as it was inexplicable and not tenable to their theory; more importantly, an examination of this core question would ultimately point to an outside creative force or intelligent designer with obvious religious implications with which they wished to avoid at all cost.

Notice that I used the word *possibility* when referring to the concept of an outside creative force. The reason is that *The Organized Universe* was explicitly designed and written to be solely scientific and *non*-religious in nature in order to legally meet the criteria developed in several Supreme Court decisions (and numerous lower court cases) which specifically excluded any hint of religiosity as a qualifier for any teachable science subject. The reasoning behind these court decisions was in keeping with the Establishment Clause of the First Amendment to the Constitution of the United States insofar as maintaining the doctrine of separation of church and state. Inherent in these rulings regarding religion was the Achilles heel of both creationists and intelligent design advocates in their attempts to inculcate their teachings into the science classroom.

However, that prohibition of the use of religion does not extend to this book, *The DNA of Scripture*. In fact, religion is the central topic, particularly that of Christianity and its Holy Scripture, and is the main reason I wrote the book. Because of the legal constraints mentioned above, we could not introduce the topic of religion into the discussion of *The Organized Universe* and remain credible as a scientific critique of evolution. With that now accomplished, we turn the focus of our attention to Chapter 4 for a detailed examination of the Holy Bible (KJV) by applying the same natural law of science that proves order and design in the universe. In doing so, we are able to reveal the hidden pattern and Devine structure of the Holy Scripture, which, by definition, proves its authenticity. This book is a unique defense of the Bible, and thus by extension that of Christianity, by providing a proof of the veracity of the Word of God in a scientific manner outside the Bible itself, which previously has not been accomplished. The authors will demonstrate that the same true natural law of science, the Law of First Digits as described in Chapters 2 and 3, when applied to the

Holy Scriptures of the Bible, proves the presence of God's unfathomable intelligence in creating and preserving the truthfulness of His Word.

Moreover, this proof extends to the identification of God as the only true God of the universe—to the exclusion of all others. That is a very powerful and controversial statement, but one that can be backed up. If one proves the entirety of the Scripture as true, then it follows that the God referred to in those same scriptures is and must be the one true God of the universe.

Admittedly, this book makes quite an assertion. It is inevitable that non-Christian believers in other religions may be offended by such an all-encompassing claim of exclusivity. We are not writing this book to be politically correct, as abhorrent as that is. However, if they believe that their particular religion and its writings have within them the power of any similar proof, then they should seek out that proof and proclaim it to the world.

As a comparison to our application to the Scriptures of the Holy Bible, you will find it most interesting when the Law of First Digits is applied to a number of the world's great religious writings. Once you understand the infallibility of 'God's measuring stick', you will be shocked at the results of their conformity or non-conformity when compared to that of the Holy Bible. The implications of the results of this "universal truth" are staggering.

The Author
Fall 2014

INTRODUCTION

The DNA of Scripture

The purpose of this book is fourfold:

1. To scientifically prove the authenticity and thereby the truth of the Holy Bible, the sacred scripture of Christianity.
2. To reveal the identity of the one true God of the universe.
3. To demonstrate that science and religion are in fact compatible and are now merging. (Until recently, most theologians considered science and religion as separate and incompatible.)
4. To prove that you cannot be an evolutionist and a Theist at the same time.

First, however, we must ask the question, Are God's Spiritual Laws compatible with His Natural Laws of the Universe?

After the publishing of Charles Darwin's Origin of Species in 1859 and the subsequent sweeping secular movement of evolution, which separated science from religion—especially that of the Christian religion and the issue of creation—we find the pendulum nearing its zenith and ready for its return trip to the truth.

The story of Darwinian evolution has been nothing short of "The Big Lie", (think Goebbels of Nazi fame) which, when told often enough becomes the "accepted truth". That "truth", however, has now been proven false (see The Organized Universe, Outskirts Press, 2013) and the act of restoring the true relationship between science and religion is now upon us.

The fact is that God's spiritual laws and His natural laws of the universe (the fundamental physical constants) are one and the same in that they are from the same divine source—the Almighty God and Creator. It is in this context that we must explore this relationship, and by so doing, find the scientific proof of this statement.

In this book we will demonstrate how true natural science confirms the Holy Scriptures as true. This will be done with a scientific proof outside of the Bible itself, which in itself is a first. We will connect the dots—the nexus if you will—by using one of God's own natural laws (the Law of First Digits in this case) to prove (with a very high probability) the authenticity of the Holy Bible (KJV). We can therefore say, if the Bible is true, then the theory of evolution cannot be; if the Bible is true, then there can be no conflict between science and religion; if the Bible is true, then science can only confirm that which is found in the Scriptures; and, lastly, if the Bible is true, then it proves that the true laws of science are also true, e.g., the Law of First Digits. Trite as it may sound, the verses in Ecclesiastes 1:9-10 state that there is nothing new under the sun. Many of the modern "scientific discoveries" were somehow already known to the inspired Biblical writers thousands of years ago. (Please see page 28 for some examples.)

This new book, *The DNA of Scripture*, is the sequel to *The Organized Universe*, in which we utilized a little known but powerful scientific law called Benford's Law of First Digits to disprove Darwinian evolution, expose the fraud of its hollow logic, and display its weak and crumbling foundation. In both books, Benford's Law commands the starring role and once again justifies its 'law of laws' title by illustrating its incredible diversity, accuracy, and flexibility as the "measuring stick of truth." In the context of this book, we call it "God's measuring stick" as it reveals its unique role in the hidden construction of the Bible.

In reviewing my research of *The Organized Universe*, I wondered what other applications conform to Benford's Law of First Digits, other than the many publicized commercial uses, that would have as great or greater impact on a major issue of our time. I theorized that if God's immutable and perfect creation contains absolute and invariant laws of nature (which it does), why would not God use one or more of these laws as a form of proof, not only as part of the construction of His Holy Scripture, but also as a device to prove the authenticity of those very same Scriptures, thus revealing Himself as the one true God of the Universe. I further surmised that if Benford's Law is omnipresent in universal matter as well as integral in everyday life events here on earth (as demonstrated in *The Organized Universe*), then Benford's Law should be the perfect law out of hundreds to test first. To my everlasting joy and amazement, my supposition paid off: there was a near perfect match. This was one of those "ah-ha" moments where the hair on the back of your neck stands up and a wave of excitement hits you full force. At this point, I knew there was no need to test any other natural laws.

The result of that one test—of counting all the significant first digit numbers in the entire 66 books of the Christian Bible and applying the statistical analysis to show the degrees of freedom and conformity—is how this book came about. It is the first of its kind using a natural law of science (outside of the Bible) as proof of the Bible as the authentic Word of God. This bridging of science and religion, a hotly divisive and contested issue today, was considered heretical by both theologians and scientists a mere 100 years ago. As there is literally nothing new under the sun, so it is with the timeless fact that science reflects God through its proof of design and vice versa. It will be shown that science and religion are indeed compatible and are now merging in many areas.

Many believe the Bible is inspired because it contains the Word of God—along with its myths, poetic hyperbole, contradictions, and legends. These people hold that it is wrong to identify the Bible as solely the Word of God; rather, they say, it is a witness of God speaking to mankind. In other words, the Word of God can be found in the Bible but the Word of God is not necessarily synonymous with the Bible. However, these two views are inadequate when the biblical evidence is considered. The Bible makes it plain that it is not merely inspiring literature or a fallible record of God speaking, *but that it is the infallible Word of God*. This book is about demonstrating and proving this very fact.

Unlike *The Organized Universe,* this book *is about religion* and science. It is about the Bible and Christianity; it is about truth and non-truth, but only in the macro sense. It is not about scriptural interpretation, denominational or inter-denominational squabbles, Hebrew or Greek translations or miss-translations, myopic contradictions taken out of context or religious arguments in general. It is simply a methodology of proof providing an extremely high probability that the Bible, as handed down over the millennia, is the authentic Word of God.

All other arguments, pro or con, stem from this very fact. If you think about it, that makes any factual argument made from the Scripture very deducible. For, as we discuss in Chapter 4, at a maximum, the conformity of the distribution of First Digit numbers to the Law of First Digits logically tells us that we can trust the remaining text of Scripture with a high level of probability.

The First Digit numbers in the Scripture are equivalent to other words in Scripture. In fact, numbers in Scripture are designated by their numerical word representation, i.e., *one, three, twenty, etc.*, not by their mathematical figure or symbol such as *1, 3, 20, etc.* Therefore, word numbers are a sampling of the total word population in Scripture.

The real question then becomes, "Is the word sampling of numbers a true representation of the other words in Scripture?" We know that in statistical quality control sampling analysis, a small random sample can represent the quality of the entire population with a very high level of probability. However, Scripture has an additional aspect in that each word is intimately related to the words adjacent to and immediately around it.

In other words, if the number is true then the phase must be true. If the phrase is true, then the sentence is true. If each sentence is true, the verse is true. If each verse is true, then the chapter is true. If each chapter is true, then the book is true. If each book is true, then the entire Scripture is true.

This leads us to the question of truth in other religions. The different religions argue their own truth based on their own sacred writings and by identifying numerous contradictions, mistranslations, incorrect definitions, context errors and incorrect facts concerning other religions. With this discord and confusion, it is almost impossible to determine which religion possesses the truth.

To penetrate this fog of confusion, what is needed is a universally agreed upon baseline or standard of truth against which to measure the veracity, or lack thereof, of the Holy Scriptures of the various world religions. We cannot use a subjective standard such as a particular religious dogma or faith as such a standard cannot be proven scientifically using the scientific method.

No one can legitimately argue against the proven natural laws of science (the fundamental physical constants of the universe) such as the Newtonian Constant of Gravitation (symbol G), which has a constant parameter of 6.673 x 10-11 m3 kg-1 s-2. As we all know, you could drop an object off a building and it will fall downward at a certain accelerated rate and hit the ground at a certain velocity every time from the same height. This truth of science has, of course, been proven by experiment after experiment. Other similar proven laws of science include the speed of light (c), mass, electron (^m_e), the electron charge (e), or the magnetic constant ($^\mu_0$) among many others.

Relatively new among these proven true laws of science is the Law of First Digits or Benford's law. Although only recently confirmed into this exclusive club of natural laws, it has the unique quality and ability to identify the natural numbers one (1) through nine (9)—both in nature and in life happenings on earth—in a particular geometric progression or distribution. If the frequency or distribution of these first significant digit numbers as found, say in the composition of matter in nature or, as in this case, in various Holy Scriptures, does not conform to the precise percentages predicted by this law, then the substance or document is not natural and is therefore false. In other words, the numbers must conform to the Law of First Digits in order to be true.

The frequency that each first significant number digit appears follows a precise mathematical formula wherein each individual number bears a certain percentage of the total population in question every time. (For example, the first significant number digit one (1) will occur approximately 30.1% of the time as opposed to the number digit nine (9) which will occur approximately 4.5% of the time.)

Therefore, using this scientific baseline or standard represents a starting point in resolving the highly contentious issue of which religion has the truth outside of faith.

Example of Proof Relating to the Holy Bible

In analyzing the Bible using the precise measurements of first significant number digits, we find total conformity even when comparing diverse books to one another. The summary results of the following six comparisons bear this out:

1. The Torah (the first five books of the Old Testament) was written by the Hand of God as dictated to Moses.
2. The Torah conforms to the Law of First Digits except for the number digit 7, which is a special exception as determined by the Torah itself and other books of the Scripture. (The number seven (7) is considered a holy number representing the word of God, perfection and completion and is examined extensively in Chapter 4.)
3. The remaining books of the Old Testament conform to the Law of First Digits with the same exception for the number digit 7.
4. When item #2 is overlaid on item # 3, there is a near perfect fit.
5. When the Gospel Books (the first four books of the New Testament and Revelation) are applied to the Law of First Digits, there is a close conformity to item #2.
6. When the remaining New Testament books are analyzed in the same manner, there is close conformity to items #2, #3, and #5.

This book is organized in the following manner:

In Chapter One, we will provide an overall approach to the book and discuss what we mean by "The DNA of Scripture" along with some fascinating background and facts concerning the Bible. We will also examine other proofs of the Bible such as Prophesy as well as non-proofs such as the now infamous equidistant letter spacing (ELS) codes.

In Chapters 2 and 3, we will discuss Benford's Law, what it is, how it went from a mere mathematical curiosity to a permanent member of an august body of natural laws of science that, among other things, are invariant over time; notable examples of these are the speed of light and the law of gravity. We will show how the relatively simple math of statistics works when applying the Law to diverse tabulated sets of natural data, both of natural phenomenon and life events on earth, and how to interpret the results, and what they mean.

In Chapter 4, the main thesis of the book is presented in detail as extrapolated from earlier chapters. We will show why Benford's Law of First Digits is actually "God's Measuring Stick". When applied to the Holy Scripture of the Bible (in this case the King James Version), it demonstrates in literally graphic fashion that the <u>entirety of the Holy Bible conforms to one of God's own laws and therefore must be His true written Word</u>. We will also discuss the anomaly of the number "7" and what its true meaning is in relation to the characterization of God. Then we will examine the question of why it actually conforms to the Benford curve when on the surface it appears not to. Furthermore, we will show that even random testing of portions of the Bible reveal surprising conformity to Benford. Examples used are the entirety of the books of both the Old Testament and the New Testament; using the Gospels, we analyzed Matthew through John + Revelation; Matthew through Acts; Matthew through Acts + Revelation; and finally, a comparison of Genesis through Deuteronomy and Matthew through John + Revelation, and other combinations. There is also a separate set of analyzes testing the number of letters, words, and first digits (as well as combinations) per different books of the Bible. You will be amazed at the results.

Knowing the results of our testing in Chapter 4, that the Holy Bible conforms to this universal law of nature and reveals it truthfulness, we then examine, in Chapter 5, the application of Benford's Law of First Digits to Scripture of the various World Religions. This will no doubt be extremely controversial to some people when you see the test results. Using the same testing methodology as with the Bible, we will seek to discover the conformity or non-conformity of such scripture as found in the Koran, The Book of Mormons, the Apocrypha of the Catholic Church, and the Tanakh—the quintessential sacred text of the Hebrew Bible. Each of these Scriptures—from the monotheistic religions to the Holy Bible—claim to reveal the truth of God. But do they? We will let you draw your own conclusions. In contrast, however, other non-monotheistic religions such as Hinduism and Buddhism have sacred texts that are considered as guides on the path to truth, not truth itself and thus do not qualify to be analyzed.

Chapter 6 will examine the application of Benford to well-known *non*-religious books and documents. These include a sampling of The Gnostic Gospels (those writings not included in the Bible but considered religious writings at the time), Dan Brown's, <u>The Da Vinci Code</u> and how the meaning of The Holy Grail was subverted and changed, Pride and Prejudice, Don Quixote, and Democracy in America by Alexis De Tocqueville, just to name a few.

In the final Chapter 7, we explore the question of Conformity and Truth and let you draw your overall conclusions from the book. What are the multiple strands of truth on which our analysis is based? What is the fourth language of the Bible after Hebrew, Aramaic, and Greek? What role does the language of mathematics play in this analysis? And finally, a re-statement of why God's invariant laws of nature, and particularly that of the First Law of Digits, play such a pivotal role in the logical conclusion that the Bible is, in fact, invariant and infallible and thus reveals the true identity of the God of the Universe and His authentic Word.

As you will see, the DNA of Scripture is not an addendum to Scripture, but is more accurately a completion as shown by the signature on digit seven (7) just as Christ is never an addendum to a scientific theory but always a *completion*. The conceptual soundness of a scientific theory cannot be maintained apart from Christ.[1]

We therefore issue the challenge to those critics who assault the trustworthiness of the Scripture by invoking the words of Dr. Robert D. Wilson in his defense of the Old Testament:

> "In conclusion, we claim that the assaults upon the integrity and trustworthiness of the Old Testament along the line of language have utterly failed. The critics have not succeeded in a single line of attack in showing that the diction and style of any part of the Old Testament are not in harmony with the ideas and aims of writers who lived at, or near, the time when the events that are recorded in the various documents... We boldly challenge these Goliaths of ex-cathedra theories to come down into the field of ordinary concordances, dictionaries, and literature, and fight a fight to the finish on the level ground of the facts

and the evidence" (Dr. Robert Dick Wilson, *A Scientific Investigation of the Old Testament* [Chicago: Moody Press, 1959], p. 130).

No one knows the full impact and future applications yet discovered of this remarkable discovery of the anomaly of numbers found everywhere in nature and in every aspect of life events, and which appears to measure truth from fiction, but we suspect you will be hearing a lot more in the near future.

The Author,

Fall 2014

CHAPTER 1

What is The DNA of Scripture?

The Holy Bible is like no other book in the entire world. It is the only book which presents itself as the written revelation of the one true God, intended for the salvation of man, and demonstrating its divine authority by many infallible proofs" **Gleason L. Archer, Jr.**[2]

Every Scripture is God-breathed (given by His inspiration) and profitable for instruction, for reproof and conviction of sin, for correction of error and discipline in obedience, [and] for training in righteousness (in holy living), in conformity to God's will in thought, purpose, and action)… 2 Timothy 3:16 **(AMPV)**

To prove something true or not is called apologetics. This word is derived from the Greek word "apologia," which means "to defend." The focus of this book is the scientific proof supporting the accuracy of the Bible. After all, if the Bible is not true or is filled with errors, Christianity would only be a "blind faith"—something people believe without any evidence to support it.

However, Christianity is not a blind faith; on the contrary, it is a realistic faith based on the true Word of God as found in the Holy Scriptures. It is also a realistic faith based on the natural senses as opposed to the mystical faith that is taught in most churches today. (This is the subject of my second book, *The 2nd Reformation: A Concerned Christian's Critical*

1

Review of the Christian Church published by Outskirts Press August 2014.) Although Christianity is the only religion that can prove itself with the main source of that proof being from within the Bible, our proof will be the first scientific proof outside the Bible.

What is the DNA of Scripture? The answer of course is God since He is the living inspiration for every God-breathed word of the Bible, just as his creation of the DNA molecule is the foundation for the design and inspiration of every living creature including man.

Just as DNA was created as a reservoir for the information of life, so the uniquely worded structure of the Bible reveals a reservoir for the salvation of life through Christ.

What is the Bible and why is it Important?

This book is written on the following two premises:

1. That the Bible is God's revelation of His will to humanity with its central thesis being that of salvation through Jesus Christ.
2. Through the use of a natural law of science outside of the Bible, we will prove the premise in # 1 above to be the authentic, true and inspired Word of God and that it is inerrant in its very structure.

If then, we prove the Bible to be true, what importance or relevance does it have to you? If it is true, then it speaks to you directly from God with the sole promise of eternal life if only you confess belief in the following:

• That Jesus came to earth as fully man in the flesh, emptied Himself of all Deity, died on the cross and was resurrected from the dead by the Holy Spirit.

What do you Know and Believe about the Bible and how do you Know it is True?

What do you really know about the Bible? You know the one—the bestselling book of all time; the one that history demonstrates has been preserved and accurately transmitted for thousands of years in spite of the many efforts to suppress, corrupt, burn and destroy it; the one that is unlike any other religious book in the world having the distinctive feature of prophesy both for nations and individuals; the one that affords the Christian religion to be the only religion that can prove itself (through the scriptures); the only one that presents itself as the written revelation of the one true God; the one that is the most influential book ever written; the one that has been translated into more languages than any other piece of literature in the world; the one whose teachings are embraced by more of the world's population than any other religion.

Yes, that is the one!

But what we are going to discuss in this book goes well beyond these distinctive features —impressive as they are; it goes beyond the offered proofs of prophesy and archeological findings and beyond any alleged hidden codes found in the Bible. It goes to the heart of any proof—*scientific proof.*

You may or may not know much about the Bible or you may or may not believe in it as true scripture from the one true God. But I will tell you, unashamedly, it is a life-changing event, a mind expanding revelation when you do discover that the Bible, the Christian Bible of the Old and New Testaments, is in fact the authentic Word of God.

A person does not have to believe in the Bible just because someone of authority—a preacher, priest, or minister—says you are supposed to; or because of peer pressure from family or friends. That is merely 'blind faith', which, strikingly, is something you do not need with Christianity because the Bible and Christianity are based on realistic faith born of proof. Remarkably, there is no other religion or holy scripture that can make that claim.

But as a rational being, you are more likely to consider a form of proof, preferably scientific proof, over any type of blind faith or third party recommendation when deciding to believe whether something is true or not. Therefore, in presenting our "proof" of the Bible, we will show a direct relationship and connection between true natural science (a natural law of science) and the Holy Scripture, which is the Holy Bible. This proof will go a long way in bridging the perceived chasm between religion and science, at least as far as Christianity and the Bible are concerned. This will show that the truth of the Holy Scripture can be proved outside of the Holy Scripture itself. To demonstrate this proof, we will use a relatively new scientific law of nature, a law that is outside of the Bible; a law that is as valid and true as any of the well-known fundamental physical constants (laws) of the universe, such as the law of gravity or the speed of light. Therein lays the uniqueness of our proof <u>that the Bible is the inspired Word of God.</u>

<u>**The Separation of True Natural Science and Religion is now over. The True God of the Universe can now be Identified.**</u>

A Sequel Using the Same Principle

As stated earlier, this book is a sequel to my first book, *The Organized Universe,* published in the fall of 2013. The reason for the sequel will become clear. In that book we used a relatively new scientific law of nature, and demonstrated, for the first time, that the overriding characteristic of the universe is defined by order, not chaos. [As related in the story of creation, the word "world" or "cosmos" (in Greek—kosmos) refers to the ordered universe of heaven and Earth]. This proof of an "ordered" or "organized" universe decimates one of the three pillars of evolution—that of natural selection which requires an early environment of chaos for its mechanism of random mutation to work. The result is that the entire foundation of Darwinian evolution is undermined and the overall theory relegated to the trash heap of history. As time passes, we believe the retrospective understanding will be that *The Organized Universe* was the final nail in the coffin of postmodern Darwinism, revealing a paradigm shift in scientific thought and the social conscience.

An important corollary to this main theme of order, upon which we will expand, is the implication that design in the universe—in all of matter and in life events here on earth—is from a supernatural or outside force.

Notice I used the word 'implication' while not explicitly stating this force to be that of God, the ultimate creator of all things.

> *"In him all things in heaven and on earth were created, things*
> *visible and invisible......All things have been created through*
> *him and for him. He himself is before all things, and in him all*
> *things hold together....." (Colossians 1:16—20* **NRSV***)*

In this book, *The DNA of Scripture,* the central theme is that if God created the universe and all within it, then he necessarily created the immutable laws of physics and the universal fundamental or physical constants that maintain what is called a fine-tuned Universe. (This concept is embedded in the Anthropic Principle, which is the proposition that the conditions that allow life in the Universe can only occur when certain universal fundamental physical constants lie within a very narrow range. If any of these constants were to differ only slightly, the Universe would unlikely be conducive to the development of matter, or life as it is presently understood. Although hotly debated among philosophers, theologians, creationists, and intelligent design proponents, it is a powerful prima fascia argument for design. However, merely establishing that there is design all around us does not tell us anything about the Designer.[3])

Consequently, our argument goes like this: if these scientific laws and universal constants are invariant (which they are) and one of these scientific laws of nature (Benford's Law of First Digits) is embedded within each of the fundamental constants and by itself proves order in the universe, why would not God use one of his proven laws to reveal the authenticity of His Word, the Holy Bible and to identify Himself as the true living God?

God and Natural Law

To crystalize this point regarding God and natural law, I would like to quote extensively from an article by Dr. Jason Lisle of Answers Magazine[4] whose thesis supports our argument precisely. It states that the universe obeys certain rules—laws to which all things must adhere. These laws are precise, and many of them are mathematical in nature. This primer on natural law will give you a solid perspective of what the laws of the universe are and how and why they work. It also helps to indirectly describe the function of Benford's Law of First Digits as a "law of laws" in that it is found in each of the separate fundamental physical constants of the universe.

An overriding statement of Creation is the law of biogenesis, which states that life always comes from life. Both observational science and Genesis 1 tell us that organisms reproduce after their own kind. This and other natural laws exist because the universe has a Creator who is logical and has imposed order on His universe.

Natural laws are hierarchical in nature; secondary laws of nature are based on primary laws of nature, which have to be just right in order for our universe to be possible. But, where did these laws come from, and why do they exist? If the universe were merely the accidental by-product of a big bang, then why should it obey orderly principles—or any principles at all for that matter? Such laws are consistent with biblical creation. Natural laws exist because the universe has a Creator God who is logical and has imposed order on His universe (Genesis 1:1).

The Word of God

Everything in the universe, every plant and animal, every rock, every particle of matter or light wave, is bound by laws which it has no choice but to obey. The Bible tells us that there are laws of nature—"ordinances of heaven and earth" (Jeremiah 33:25). What a beautiful phrase— "ordinances of heaven and earth". If that does not describe the immutable and invariant "laws of the universe", I do not know what would. These laws describe the way God normally accomplishes His will in the universe.

God's logic is built into the universe, and so the universe is not haphazard or arbitrary, it is to say again, ordered. It obeys laws of chemistry that are logically derived from the laws of physics, many of which can be logically derived from other laws of physics and laws of mathematics. The most fundamental laws of nature exist only because God wills them to; they are the logical, orderly way that the Lord upholds and sustains the universe He has created. The atheists (and evolutionists for that matter) are unable to account for the logical, orderly state of the universe. Why should the universe obey laws if there is no law-giver? But laws of nature are perfectly consistent with biblical creation. In fact, the Bible is the foundation for natural laws.

The Law of Life (Biogenesis)

As we stated above, the law of biogenesis states simply that life always comes from life. This is what observational science tells us: organisms reproduce other organisms after their own kind. Historically, Louis Pasteur disproved one alleged case of spontaneous generation; he showed that life comes from previous life. Since then, we have seen that this law is universal—with no known exceptions. This is, of course, exactly what we would expect from the Bible. According to Genesis 1, God supernaturally created the first diverse kinds of life on earth and made them to reproduce after their kind. Notice that molecules-to-man evolution violates the law of biogenesis. Evolutionists believe that life (at least once) spontaneously formed from nonliving chemicals. But this is inconsistent with the law of biogenesis. Real science confirms the Bible.

Everything in the Universe, Every Plant and Animal, Every Rock, Every Particle of Matter or Light Wave, is Bound by Laws which it has no Choice but to Obey.

The Laws of Chemistry

Life requires a specific chemistry. Our bodies are powered by chemical reactions and depend on the laws of chemistry operating in a uniform fashion. Even the information that makes up any living being is stored on a long molecule called DNA. Life as we know it would not be possible if the laws of chemistry were different. God created the laws of chemistry in just the right way so that life would be possible.

The laws of chemistry give different properties to the various elements (each made of one type of atom) and compounds (made up of two or more types of atoms that are bonded together) in the universe. For example,

7

when given sufficient activation energy, the lightest element (hydrogen) will react with oxygen to form water. Water itself has some interesting properties, such as the ability to hold an unusually large amount of heat energy. When frozen, water forms crystals with six-sided symmetry (which is why snowflakes are generally six-sided). Contrast this with salt (sodium chloride) crystals, which tend to form cubes. It is the six-fold symmetry of water ice that causes "holes" in its crystal, making it less dense than its own liquid. That's why ice floats in water (whereas essentially all other frozen compounds sink in their own liquid).

The properties of elements and compounds are not arbitrary. In fact, the elements can be logically organized into a periodic table based on their physical properties. Substances in the same column on the table tend to have similar properties. This follows because elements in a vertical column have the same outer electron structures. These outermost electrons determine the physical characteristics of the atom. The periodic table did not happen by chance. Atoms and molecules have their various properties because their electrons are bound by the laws of quantum physics. In other words, chemistry is based on physics. If the laws of quantum physics were just a bit different, atoms might not even be possible. God designed the laws of physics just right so that the laws of chemistry would come out the way He wanted them to.

The Laws of Planetary Motion

The creation scientist Johannes Kepler discovered that the planets in our solar system obey three laws of nature. He found that planets orbit in ellipses (not perfect circles as had been previously thought) with the sun at one focus of the ellipse; thus a given planet is sometimes closer to the sun than at other times. Kepler also found that planets sweep out equal areas in equal times—in other words, planets speed up as they get closer to the sun within their orbit. And third, Kepler found the exact mathematical relationship between a planet's distance from the sun (a) and its orbital period (p); planets that are farther from the sun take much longer to orbit than planets that are closer (expressed as $p^2=a^3$). Kepler's laws also apply to the orbits of moons around a given planet.

As with the laws of chemistry, these laws of planetary motion are not fundamental. Rather, they are the logical derivation of other laws of nature. In fact, it was another creation scientist (Sir Isaac Newton) who discovered that Kepler's laws could be derived mathematically from certain laws of physics—specifically, the laws of gravity and motion (which Newton himself formulated).

The Laws of Physics

The field of physics describes the behavior of the universe at its most fundamental level. There are many different laws of physics. They describe the way the universe operates today. Some laws of physics describe how light propagates, how energy is transported, how gravity operates, how mass moves through space, and many other phenomena. The laws of physics are usually mathematical in nature; some laws of physics can be described with a concise formula, such as $E=mc^2$. The simple formula $F=ma$ shows how an object with mass (m) will accelerate (a) when a net force (F) is applied to it. It is amazing that every object in the universe consistently obeys these rules.

There is a hierarchy in physics: some laws of physics can be derived from other laws of physics. For example, Einstein's famous formula $E=mc^2$ (energy = mass x the speed of light squared) can be derived from the principles and equations of special relativity. *Conversely, there are many laws of physics that cannot be derived from other laws of physics; many of these are suspected to be derivative principles, but scientists have not yet deduced their derivation.* Emphasis added.

And some laws of physics may be truly fundamental (not based on other laws); they exist only because God wills them to. In fact, this must be the case for at least one law of physics (and perhaps several)—the most fundamental. (Logically, this is because if the most fundamental law were based on some other law, it would not be the most fundamental law.)

The laws of physics (along with their associated constants) are fine-tuned in just the right way so that life, particularly human life, is possible. This fact is called the "anthropic principle"[5] and was defined on page 5.

The Laws of Mathematics

Notice that the laws of physics are highly mathematical in nature. They would not work if there were not also laws of mathematics. Mathematical laws and principles include the rules of addition, the transitive property, the commutative properties of addition and multiplication, the binomial theorem, and many others. Like the laws of physics, some laws and properties of mathematics can be derived from other mathematical principles. But unlike the laws of physics, the laws of mathematics are abstract; they are not "attached" to any specific part of the universe. It is possible to imagine a universe where the laws of physics are different, but it is difficult to imagine a (consistent) universe where the laws of mathematics are different.

The laws of mathematics are an example of a "transcendent truth." They must be true regardless of what kind of universe God created. This may be because God's nature is logical and mathematical; thus, any universe He chose to create would necessarily be mathematical in nature. The secular naturalist cannot account for the laws of mathematics. Certainly he would believe in mathematics and would use mathematics, but he is unable to account for the existence of mathematics within a naturalistic framework since mathematics is not a part of the physical universe. However, the Christian understands that there is a God beyond the universe and that mathematics reflects the thoughts of the Lord. Understanding math is, in a sense, "thinking God's thoughts after Him"[6] (though in a limited, finite way, of course).

Some have supposed that mathematics is a human invention. It is said that if human history had been different, an entirely different form of math would have been constructed—one with alternate laws, theorems, axioms, etc. But such thinking is not consistent. Are we to believe that the universe did not obey mathematical laws before people discovered them? Did the planets orbit differently before Kepler discovered that $p^2=a^3$? *Clearly, mathematical laws are something that human beings have discovered, not invented* (Emphasis added). The only thing that might have been different (had human history taken a different course) is the notation—the way in which we choose to express mathematical truths through symbols. But these truths exist regardless of how they are expressed. Mathematics could rightly be called the "language of creation." As you will see later on, we show this "language" to be the fourth language of the Bible.

The Laws of Logic

All the laws of nature, from physics and chemistry to the law of biogenesis, depend on the laws of logic. Like mathematics, the laws of logic are transcendent truths. We cannot imagine that the laws of logic could be anything different from what they are. Take the law of non-contradiction for example. This law states that you cannot have both "A" and "not A" at the same time and in the same relationship. Without the laws of logic, reasoning would be impossible. But where do the laws of logic come from?

The atheist cannot account for the laws of logic, even though he or she must accept that they exist in order to do any rational thinking. But according to the Bible, God is logical. Indeed, the law of non-contradiction reflects God's nature; God cannot lie (Numbers 23:19) or be tempted with evil (James 1:13) since these things contradict His perfect nature. Since we have been made in God's image, we instinctively know the laws of logic. We are able to reason logically (though because of finite minds and sin we do not always think entirely logically).

The Uniformity of Nature

The laws of nature are uniform and invariant. They do not (arbitrarily) change, and they apply throughout the whole cosmos. The laws of nature apply in the future just as they have applied in the past; this is one of the most basic assumptions in all of science. Without this assumption, science would be impossible. If the laws of nature suddenly and arbitrarily changed tomorrow, then past experimental results would tell us nothing about the future. Why is it that we can depend on the laws of nature to apply consistently throughout time? The secular scientists cannot justify this important assumption. But the Christian can because the Bible gives us the answer. God is Lord over all creation and sustains the universe in a consistent and logical way. God does not change, and so He upholds the universe in a consistent, uniform way throughout time (Jeremiah 33:25). (Another description of "order,")

Conclusion

We have seen that the laws of nature depend on other laws of nature, which ultimately depend on God's will. Thus, God created the laws of physics in just the right way so that the laws of chemistry would be correct, so that life can exist. It is doubtful that any human would have been able to solve such a complex puzzle. Yet, the Lord has done so. The atheist cannot account for these laws of nature (even though he agrees that they must exist), for such laws are inconsistent with naturalism. Yet, they are perfectly consistent with the Bible. We expect the universe to be organized in a logical, orderly fashion and to obey uniform laws because the universe was created by the power of God.

Now back to the fundamental question at hand—is the Bible the true Word of God or not?

Certainly, others have tried to answer this question but with differing measures of success. The perpetual controversy continues. Our approach and logic is very simple:

> If it can be shown that the natural laws of the universe (the fundamental physical constants in particular) and the natural laws of science as discussed above, all of which are invariant as to time, were created by God at the moment of creation, then by logical extension, the Bible—his revealed Word—would also have to conform to His own law. Therefore, the very proof of this assumption will then demonstrate the Bible to be the actual inspired Word of God, extended by definition to be infallible as to every word.

The scientific tool used in this proof is called Benford's Law of First Digits, a relatively new and obscure natural law of science, which, as stated

12

above, has the same validity and weight as the fundamental physical constants of the universe, such as the Newtonian constant of gravitation, the speed of light in vacuum, magnetic constant, or the electric constant. In other words, it has a very strong pedigree.

Therefore, if the above proves true, then the only conclusion one can draw is that the Bible is in harmony with God's natural laws and is therefore authenticated as the written Word or God as advertised.

What a profound revelation around which to wrap one's mind.

Other Proofs

You might ask why this proof is necessary. Are there not abundant proofs of the Bible already in existence? The short answer is no. Even in light of other proofs, we believe this proof is unique and necessary for three reasons:

1. To counter the ongoing and unrelenting assault on the authority of the Bible by the so-called "intellectual/atheists elite" and others.[7] To demonstrate for the first time a scientific proof of the Bible lying outside of the Bible itself.
2. To make a clear and dramatic statement of proof so that skeptics and non-believers may become curious (or shocked) enough to take a second look and ask how and why this is possible. It is just possible they may discover the life-altering message of salvation contained in the Bible. For after all, that is the main purpose of Christianity—to get the message out about salvation.

Over the course of the book, we will provide you with answers to the following questions and more:

- *Is the Bible the truly inspired word of God? (shown with our proof)*
- *Is the Bible only a collection of myths, legends and contradictions and therefore not a trustworthy source of historical, theological or scientific information?(shown with our proof)*

- *Was the Bible preserved for thousands of years in its original form, translated without errors from original manuscripts? Must be if our proof holds.*
- *Is the Bible's instruction for humanity relevant today?*
- *Is there an invisible hand of God that controls the natural and spiritual aspects of the universe and planet earth?*

Of course, the simple answer is that if the Bible is proved to be true, then the answer to question #1 is yes and the answer to all other questions becomes self-evident.

This book, *The DNA of Scripture,* is not the first or is it the last of the many evidences that prove (or purport to prove) that the Bible is truly the inspired Word of God. For example, there are those who claim to have found hidden codes in the orthodox Masoretic Hebrew text of the Old Testament revealing supposed prophesy of future events. There are the numerous prophesies regarding individuals and nations of the Bible that have been predicted and ultimately fulfilled. There are those intellectual conclusions derived from theology such as intelligent design and theistic evolution who try to put a fine point on equivocation to support their position. There are manuscript evidences unearthed in recent times (E.g., the Dead Sea Scrolls) that conform to the original ancient texts of the Gospels, and there are those individuals who, through proof of numerous historical documents, were alive at the time of Christ and the subsequent gospel writings that are reflected in recorded history. And the list goes on.

Scientific Proofs in the Bible

There are many instances referenced in the Bible where the writers have indeed demonstrated advanced scientific knowledge with incredible accuracy and foreknowledge. The following is to name but a few: [8]

- Man was formed from the dust of the ground (Genesis 2:7). Today, scientists have confirmed that every single element found in the clay and dirt of the ground is contained in the human body.

- Creation of the Universe
  - ○ Virtually all scientists now agree that the universe was created in the 'Big Bang' at a specific point in time. The universe had a beginning just as God said. (Genesis 1:1)
  - ○ The waters above the firmament: God divided the waters from below the firmament from those above the firmament (Genesis 1:6-7). Today we know that massive amounts of water do exist in outer space, from the ice caps on Mars, from the rings of Saturn to the trillions of frozen comets in the Oort cloud at the edge of our solar system.
- The Coming of Christ in both day and night (Luke 17); knowledge of the earth's orbital properties around the sun.
- The Seven Stars of Pleiades — there were only 6 stars visible to the naked eye until modern telescopes were able to detect a seventh star. (Amos 5:8)

There are many other examples. How could these writers have known this advanced knowledge of science unless God supernaturally inspired them? Of course they were inspired. Because of God's omnipresence (in the past, present and future at once), these examples were to become self-revealing in our modern, scientific world and obviously demonstrate His knowledge and the inspired prophecies of the writers. However, they do not reflect on the overall truth of the Bible in its entirety, only the accuracy of certain statements made some 2500 years ago.

In contrast, you will see that our 'scientific proof' appends to the entirety of the Bible as to its trustworthiness as the authentic Word of God. *It is unique in that it does not reference itself in the Bible per se*; nor does it manifest itself in events past or future or become inferred from signs or miracles. It simply reveals itself as being integral to the very fabric and construction of the Bible in such a way as to identically reflect the preciseness and invariability of the very laws of nature that God Himself created at the moment of Creation.

> *(John 1:1—3) "In the beginning was the Word, and Word was with God, and the Word was God. He was in the beginning with God. All things came into being by Him,*

15

> *and apart from Him nothing came into being that has come into being. Also see (Malachi 3:6) "I am the LORD, I change not" and (James 1:17) "...there is no variableness, neither shadow of turning"*

In other words, God's design is perfect and immutable and this perfection is reflected in all his works including, as we will show, his inspired Word. This all-encompassing truth becomes breathtaking in its scope when you consider the unfathomable complexity of a universal design that incorporates a simple pattern of "order" in the construction of everything from the molecular structure of matter—including our very own DNA—to the very words of the Bible. Therefore, if this is true, then the Bible, as passed down to us over the millennia, should conform to God's own natural laws including that of the Law of First Digits.

In *The Organized Universe*, we undertook the herculean task of disproving Darwin's godless Theory of Evolution using the same powerful scientific tool, Benford's Law of First Digits. This proof shatters the last vestige of hope evolutionists have in perpetuating a flawed and fraudulent theory, a theory thoroughly engrained in mainstream thought thereby undermining the truth of creation and the _true_ origin of life. When fully exposed and understood among both scientists and laymen, *The Organized Universe* will undoubtedly create a model shift in how the theory of evolution has been viewed over the last 150 plus years. (A brief synopsis of this book can be found in the Appendixes.)

By comparison, we will also show that our use of this obscure scientific law (the Law of First Digits) reveals a unique and fundamental pattern or order not found in any other written work, religious or otherwise. This again proves the unique truthfulness of His Word as contained in the Holy Bible thus revealing God's identity as the one true God.

Why the analogy to DNA?

Think of DNA as the building block and blueprint of life. It is found in the makeup of our genes that is in the nucleus of every cell of every living organism. Technically, it is one of two long chemical polymers composed of an incredibly complex amalgam of amino acids and a sugar, a phosphate group, and a base that are self-replicating in the production of proteins and much more. If a single DNA strand residing in one of the 26 pairs of chromosomes within the cell nucleus were unraveled, it would be approximately 6 feet long; if all the strands of DNA in your body were stretched end to end, they would reach to the moon and back.

This complexity of DNA can be more easily appreciated if we examine the astonishing complexity of a single cell.[9] Today, we know that the simplistic assumptions made back in Darwin's time are no longer valid. We know that a single cell with a nucleus is the microscopic equivalent of an entire high-tech, industrialized city. A wall, armed with a tight security system, selectively allowing raw materials to enter and manufactured products to leave surrounds it. The city contains a factory in production around the clock, tied to a trillion other similar factories by a mysterious communications network that dictates repair schedules and keeps track of all inventory.

A special library within each city is filled with detailed blueprints for every piece of machinery and maintenance equipment it uses. In living organisms, this information includes every minute characteristic of the organism, from the number hairs on a human body to the shape, size, and function of every organ, including the unique pattern of each fingerprint for example.

Directions for all of this activity are encoded in DNA, the genetic material of each cell that is wound into the shape of a double helix within the microscopically small nucleus. DNA also supplies detailed instructions on how to make and distribute all the necessary complex proteins that organisms need to use as building materials and as enzymes to carry out millions of functions that keep the host organism alive and healthy. This process is called protein synthesis, a highly sophisticated, intricately designed process that takes place trillions of times a day within the cells of a human body.

To make matters even more complicated, the "language" of DNA is expressed in chemicals that are called nucleotides, and the "language" of proteins is expressed in chemical complexes called amino acids. To manufacture proteins, a translation from one language to the other is necessary. This is where the RNA (ribonucleic acid) molecules come in. They translate the four nucleotides of DNA into the twenty amino acids used to build proteins. These twenty amino acids combine in unique configurations to product thousands of proteins. [10]

The connection here is that both DNA and the Bible are, in their basic form, "information systems" upon which the ultimate outcome of their purpose is manifest in the truth they each behold. In other words, the "ordered design" inherent in DNA forestalls any random act of capricious fate in the development of any organism and instead guides the immensely complex cellular biology toward its intended end result; likewise, the Bible, as an information system on one level, rests on a supernatural ordered "instruction manual" containing exceedingly great and precious promises that enable humanity to participate in the divine nature of God.

DNA is God's miraculous coding instruction for the development and growth within every species of life on earth. As the Law of Biogenesis states above, the Bible tells us in Genesis Chapter 1 that each created kind of plant and animal was coded to reproduce just its own kind.

> *"Can the fig tree, my brethren, bear olives, or a grapevine, figs? Neither can a salt spring furnish fresh water".* (James 3:12) **AMPV**

This same theme is reiterated in the New Testament in Paul's great chapter on death and resurrection.

> *God given it a body as it hath pleased him, and to every seed its own body. All flesh is not the same flesh: but there is one kind of flesh for men, another flesh of beasts, another of fishes, and another of birds"* (1 Corinthians 15:38—39).

An oak tree cannot become an apple tree any more than a fish can evolve into a man. The uniqueness to their identities is in their DNA.

In a similar manner, the Holy Scripture of the Bible contains not only the uniqueness to its own identity and that of God, but also all the necessary knowledge and instruction for humanity—from the history of the creation of the Universe, of Man, to the redemption and salvation of our souls and everything in between.

"All Scripture is God-breathed and is useful for teaching, rebuking, correcting, and training in righteousness, so that the man of God may be thoroughly equipped for every good work." (2 Timothy 3:16-17)

<u>If it is "God-breathed", then it is self-contained and perfect in design and content. The point being that the Bible is the self-contained Word of God just as is the tiny but incredibly intricate code contained in a strand of DNA.</u> As we will demonstrate in Chapter 4, the Bible contains the hidden genetic information by its Maker, which identifies the uniqueness and authenticity of this one-of-a-kind sacred Scripture. As we stated, no other religious scripture can boast this quality.

The Bible acts as a generational repeating instruction manual for humanity with its proven accuracy of history, prophesy, moral and practical lessons for daily living, health, marriage, death and, most importantly, a recipe for ever-lasting life. This statement is only true, however, if, and only if, the Bible is proven to be the authentic and infallible Word of God. Otherwise, it is just another religious text of opinions of some ancient writers proving naysayers right by default.

Therefore, the central question is, how do we know if the Bible is true and represents the unquestionable Word of God as written down over a period of thousands of years by divinely inspired apostles? *Is there a scientific way to prove its authenticity?*

The not surprising answer is a resounding **YES.**

This revelation not only proves the authenticity of Scripture but also reveals the true identity of God.

In chapters 2 and 3, we will explain the Law of First Digits in detail with numerous examples as applied to both the natural world and life events here on earth. We will then show in Chapter 4 the flawless inter-connection between the embedded design of the law in nature and life events and in the immutable, inerrant Word of God as recorded in the Holy Scripture (KJV). Since this subject of the Bible and its myriad controversies and implications is so vast, we will focus narrowly on the actual proof and what this should mean to average person, Christian or non-believer. This is not a book of Bible instruction or interpretation but merely one of proof regarding its authenticity.

The Bible, unlike any other religious scripture, conforms to this true natural law of the universe, which is essentially a pattern hidden in plain sight. However, you will be fitted with those very special "viewing glasses" that will show you where to look and how to interpret the numbers according to scientific analysis. Think of this law simply as a "measuring stick." We use many different scales of measurement to quantify everything from the length, width, and depth of a piece of furniture to the time it takes light to go to the nearest star and back. Scientific measurement is the quantification of data in an experiment and is now accurate down to the precise measurement of the molecular weight, size and density of a nanoparticle in a single procedure of ultracentrifugation.

> **We, therefore, proclaim the measuring stick for God's handiwork—whether the creation of a fathomless universe, or life and Man, or His inspired Word found in the Holy Bible—is the Law of First Digits.**

This "pattern", which is permanently embedded into every particle of matter reflecting the perfect order of creation is not there by chance we assert, but by the hand of God from the very instant of creation in which the fundamental elements of our universe (beams of light and later hydrogen and helium and the heavier elements) and the resulting fundamental physical constants (and their associated natural laws) were created. This pattern or orderly array is part of God's design not just for the Bible but for everything—from the universe to the smallest sub-atomic particle to the inspired writings of both the Old and New Testaments of the Bible.

> **We believe this remarkable revelation is the definitive proof above all others of our Creator's unique identity as the One True Living God.**

Inspiration for Writing

Among other reasons for writing my first book, *The Organized Universe*, I decided to take the advice of C. S. Lewis[11] who encouraged Christians to write books about science that would counter the materialist worldview implicitly by presenting "perfectly honest science". This was accomplished by using the Law of First Digits to disprove the godless Theory of Evolution as espoused by Charles Darwin and his subsequent modern day apologists. In the same vein, I am continuing that trend in this book by using the same science to prove the authenticity of the Bible as being the Word of God as handed down in both the Old and New Testaments. An additional reason for writing both of these books is well stated by Grant R. Jeffrey[12]:

> For almost seventeen centuries from the time of Emperor Constantine's conversion in A.D. 300 until the beginning of our century, the Bible was generally accepted by Western culture as the inspired and authoritative Word of God. However, we have witnessed an unrelenting assault on the authority of the Bible by the [so-called] intellectual elite, the academic community, liberal theologians, and the media during the last hundred years. Most people in our culture have been exposed to countless attacks on the authority and accuracy of the Scriptures in high schools and universities and from the mass media.

Proof in Bible Codes?

However, Jeffery goes on to say he believes that God has provided the extraordinary new evidence of what are called the Bible Codes[13] to prove to this generation of skeptics that the Bible is truly the inspired Word of God. We wholeheartedly disagree. We believe that God has provided the extraordinary new evidence (and proof) of the Bible's divinity through its conformity to The Law of First Digits, a universal true natural law of science, proving that there is an immutable order and detectable pattern to everything God has created *including his Holy Word*. With all deference to Mr. Jeffrey, the Law of First Digits was not widely known at the time of his writing and only now, with the publishing of our first two books, has there been any provable relationship between this true natural law of science, God's creation of man and universe, and his Holy Word. Nonetheless, many scientists and writers have since debunked any and all of the Bible Code books, notably one by Michael Drosnin.[14]

To illustrate the infallibility of God's consistency in his design as reflected in the Law of First Digits, a short discussion of the above mentioned Bible Code is instructive. As appealing as these codes first appeared, a short comparison between these equidistant letter sequence (ELS) Bible Codes and the Law of First Digits as our true measuring stick will reveal our skepticism as to any proof offered by these "codes" concerning the authenticity of the Bible.

Some of the examples of purported events foretold by these 3,000-year-old codes found embedded only in the Old Testament are:

- The Kennedy Assassination
- The Oklahoma City Bombing
- The Election of Bill Clinton
- Events from WWII
- Watergate
- The Atomic Bomb on Hiroshima
- The Moon Landing
- The Collision of a comet with Jupiter

In a few cases, detailed predictions were 'found in advance' and the events then happened exactly as predicted. One dramatic example was the assassination of Prime Minister Yitzhak Rabin, which reference was uncovered 1 year prior to the assassination.

Despite all the commotion and publicity first attributed to these Bible codes as a revelation from God, a comparison to the precision of how the Holy Scripture follows the Law of First Digits is revealing. Using that analogy to the application to the ELS Bible Code, the code would have to conform to the following observations in order to equal the scientific status of any true natural law of science and thus be credible:

- ❖ The ELS Bible Code would have to begin with a designated starting point, the first letter in Genesis 1:1for example, or some other non-arbitrary point and then skip exactly a predetermined number of letters throughout the entire Torah. These parameters should be determined prior to any application to the text. They should not be variables as they are now used.

❖ This determination of the exact number of letters (a non-variable) to be skipped and the exact starting point must also be a universal true natural law of science.

❖ Any and all the secret coded messages revealed would have to come from only those designated EDS letters.

❖ This universal true natural law of science must also be able to measure true real life happenings and events and the true physical arrangement or order of nature.

❖ The ELS Bible Code should apply equally to the entirety of the Old and New Testaments of the Bible, not just to the Torah and the Book of Isaiah.

Statistically, the ELS code is only one of the many millions of possible sequences available. Finding a particular sequence here and there to accomplish the partial goals of the Bible Code is insignificant and insufficient as any form of proof.

The DNA of Scripture offers proof that all Scripture is uniformly the truth, *not just the Torah.* The fact that the Bible Code does not work for all Scripture is additional proof of its invalidity.

Moreover, it would seem strange that God's prophetic Word would be open only to the computer literate since a special computer program is required to reveal these codes. So if the entire Bible is the authentic Word of God (as we will prove), the so called Bible Codes are in direct conflict with the following passage from II Peter 1:19-21 where the Word of God cautions that *"no prophecy of the Scripture is of any private interpretation."* In other words, prophecy is not the private province of any person by virtue of a special and unique method of interpretation.

Furthermore, any man-made coding system cannot be revealed to the author by God because *""the natural (unsaved) man receiveth not the things of the Spirit of God: for they are foolishness unto him; neither can he know them, because they are spiritually discerned"* (I Corinthians 2:14).

These shortcomings will become evident in Chapters 2 and 3 as we examine the mathematical formula and various applications of the Law of First Digits.

Moreover, unlike the complex codes described in the Bible Code revelations mentioned above and in other recently published books, the "code" we speak of (Law of First Digits) does not require high-speed computers to analyze and re-analyze various letter spacing or complex sequencing until there is a "hit". Instead, the numbers analyzed by the Law of First Digits are hidden in plain sight and can be analyzed by simply counting the significant leading digits one through nine (1-9) as they occur in the written text. [In fact, in my original research, I hand counted each number in both the Old and New Testaments as I came across them and simply made a tally of each number. A sample of my original analysis appears in the Appendixes. As an interesting side note and spur of the moment experiment, when I tallied the number of first significant digits in both the Old and New Testaments, and divided each total by the number of actual letters in each testament (these numbers are publicly available), *the proportional percentage relationship was exactly the same* (within 41 decimal points). This is more than just a coincidence for it reflects the consistency of proportionality found in the Law of First Digits including its unique logarithmic distribution of the digits. You can see the analysis in Chapter 4.]

Also in Chapter 4, you will see that we use simple statistical formulae to analyze these tallies of leading significant digits to determine their conformity or not to Benford's Law of First Digits. Since my original research was in fact done manually by counting each word number, we have since developed proprietary software designed to scan a written document (in text format) and calculate the occurrence of the actual first significant digits (again disregarding the number "0" and any decimal point) in a much faster and efficient manner. This necessitated software code to not only identify a qualifying number (one, six, fifteen, three hundred, etc. and then determine the first significant digit) but to exclude embedded numbers in the language (any*one* for tennis), pronouns (*One* should know better), chapter, verse and page numbers, and other anomalies of modern language. Remember, the inclusion of verses and chapters and page numbers of the Bible are manmade. The original manuscripts were not formatted but continuous. Nevertheless, our analysis shows that even with these modern formatting techniques, the Bible still conforms to Benford.

Thus, not only is my original research verified, but also this newly developed proprietary software can now be used in a wide variety of similar applications. Initially, we are researching to determine whether or not a wide variety of documents conform to the law. This leads to some interesting findings as we will discuss in Chapters 6 and 7. We will let you draw your own conclusions from this comparison.

CHAPTER 2

What is Benford's Law of First Digits and what does it Prove

"God is in the Details"
Ludwig Mies Van Der Rohe, 1959.

"Numbers are the World's Wonders"
Sophocles (495-405 B.C.)

Consider the following big picture prose, deftly describing this universal phenomenon known as Benford's Law of First Digits:

> Amid the swirling chaos of our world, an almost perfect pattern surrounds. It connects random events and phenomena—from the large to the small, and the monumental to the inconsequential.[15]

This comprehensive description embodies the universal patterns found in Benford's law: from mathematics to stock prices, from the elements of seawater to the random lengths of rivers and countless other examples.

This unexpected quirk in our number system was identified by an obscure mathematical rule first discovered in the late 19th century and then quickly forgotten. Today the law, known as Benford's Law, is revealing even more remarkable relationships from the physical sciences to the veracity of the printed word.

Other researchers are likewise amazed when they discover that the digits of numbers related to natural events are not uniform but distributed in a specific way, i.e., the natural world is littered with a surplus of numbers starting with the digit one. "Most physicists would think that the likelihood of a number beginning with a one (1) would occur just as often with numbers beginning with a two (2) or a three (3), and so on," says Professor Malcolm Sambridge from the Research School of Earth Sciences. "But it turns out this is not the case in the natural world. Instead, as the theory shows, roughly 30 percent of numbers related to many real-world events begin with the number one and only 17 per cent begin with a two. And it goes right down to roughly about four per cent beginning with a nine (9)."[16]

Table 1. Theoretical logarithmic law (the number zero cannot be the first significant digit).

First digit	1	2	3	4	5	6	7	8	9
Frequency %	*30.1*	*17.6*	*12.5*	*9.7*	*7.9*	*6.7*	*5.8*	*5.1*	*4.6*

Background

Major discoveries come in unusual ways. Sometimes that are discovered, forgotten and then found again. Such is the case of Benford's Law of First Digits.

Before it was called Benford's law, it was just a curious observation by an astronomer and mathematician named Simon Newcomb in 1881. Thus the story begins.

Who was Simon Newcomb?[17] A remarkable man as you will see. Born in March of 1835 in Nova Scotia, Canada he did not receive a formal education, but he showed a remarkable aptitude for mathematics at an early age. He learned to count at age four and was spending several hours a day performing addition and multiplication problems by age five. Newcomb learned to extract cube roots by the time he was seven. At 16, he apprenticed with a "quack herb doctor" and began to study mathematics after moving to Maryland in 1854.

Newcomb spent many of his hours studying mathematics and astronomy at the library. He was particularly interested in the American Ephemeris and

Nautical Almanac, an annual handbook for astronomers that contained the predicted positions in the sky of the principal celestial objects and other astronomical phenomena. Shortly thereafter, he secured employment performing mathematical computations for the American Nautical Almanac Office in Cambridge, Massachusetts. He eventually graduated from the Lawrence Scientific School of Harvard University in 1858.

He was appointed to the Naval Observatory Washington in 1861 and received a commission in the Corps of Professors of Mathematics in United States Navy. In 1877 he became the Director of the American Nautical Office and started studying the constraints of the astronomy and the calculations of the motions of the bodies in the solar system. The tables developed by Newcomb were used throughout the world to calculate the daily position of celestial objects from 1901 to 1959. Hardly anything in the tables has proven to be incorrect as of the end of the 20th century.

Newcomb's Observation

In 1881 Newcomb noted a strange phenomenon while examining his logarithm book. Logarithm books were used by scientists and mathematicians to multiply and divide large numbers before the advent of calculators and computers. One simply looked up the logarithms (in the log book) for each of the two numbers that you wanted to multiply, added the logarithms together, looked up the anti-logarithm of that number and that was your answer.

Newcomb observed that the first few pages of his logarithm book were more worn and dirtier than the other pages. Since the first few pages of a logarithm book lists multi-digit logs beginning with the digits 1, 2, and 3, Newcomb theorized that scientists spent more time dealing with logs that began with 1, 2, or 3. He also found that for each succeeding number the amount of time decreases. For example, less time was spent on 4 than 5 and less time on 5 than 6, and so forth.

Newcomb's Analysis

From this observation, Newcomb theorized that a multi-digit number is more likely to begin with the digit 1, 2, or 3. He devised a formula to explain the observation: the probability of a number beginning with digit X is equal to $\log_{10}(1 + (1/x)$. There will be more on this formula later.

Based upon his observation, Newcomb wrote "Note on the Frequency of Use of the Different Digits in Natural Numbers" which appeared in the *American Journal of Mathematics*.

Newcomb's theory went widely unnoticed by mathematicians primarily because he failed to provide a reason why his formula worked or the statistical basis for his theories. In addition, his discovery did not appear to have any practical application.

Newcomb continued to work at the American Nautical Almanac Office, and in 1884, he obtained an additional appointment of Professor of Mathematics Astronomy, which he held until 1893. He became the editor of the Journal of Mathematics and a founder of the American Astronomical Society. He died in July of 1909.

So, what did Newcomb actually discover? That the ten digits do not occur with equal frequency must be evident to anyone making much use of logarithmic tables, and noticing how much faster the first pages wear out than the last ones.

It was not until 1938 when Frank Benford's article appeared in the *Proceedings of the American Philosophical Society*, that scientists paid more attention to this phenomenon. Benford, a physicist at General Electric, somehow "rediscovered" this phenomenon and so the law took his name at the expense of Newcomb. The interesting part is that Benford begins his paper by making the same observation as did Newcomb: that the first few pages of a book of common logarithms show more wear than the last pages. This is a key point. Benford's actual 'rediscovery' and subsequent analysis are best described by Mark J. Nigrini, Ph.D. in one of his earlier publications on using Benford's Law for digital analysis:[18]

Benford's Law

Benford's Law gives the expected frequencies of the digits in tabulated data. The phenomenon is named after Frank Benford, a physicist who published the seminal paper on the topic (Benford, 1938). Contrary to intuition, the digits are not all equally likely and exhibit a heavily biased skewedness in favor of the lower digits.

Benford begins his paper by noting that the first few pages of a book of common logarithms show more wear than the last pages. From this he concludes that the first few pages were used more often than the last few pages. The common feature of the data from the first few pages is that they gave the logs of numbers with low first digits (e.g., 1, 2, and 3). He hypothesized that this was because most of the "use" numbers had a low first digit. The first digit is the leftmost digit in a number and, for example, the first digit of 110,364 is a 1. Zero is inadmissible as a first digit leaving nine possible first digits (1, 2... 9).

Benford then analyzed the first digits of two lists of numbers with a total of 20,229 records. He made an effort to collect data from as many fields as possible and to include a variety of widely different types of data sets. The data varied from random numbers having no relationship to each other, such as the numbers from the front pages of newspapers and all the numbers in an issue of Reader's Digest, to formal mathematical tabulations such as mathematical tables and scientific constants. Other data sets included the drainage areas of rivers, population numbers, American league statistics, and street numbers from an issue of American Men of Science. Benford either analyzed the entire data set at hand or in the case of large data sets to the point that he was assured that he had a fair average. The latter statement suggests that the work was time consuming. The shortest list (atomic weights) had 91 records and the largest list had 5,000 records.

Benford's results showed that on average 30.6 percent of the numbers had a first digit 1, 18.5 percent of the numbers had a first digit 2, and 4.7 percent had a first digit 9. Benford then observed a pattern to his results. He noted that the actual proportion for the first digit 1 was approximately equal to the common logarithm of 2 or 2/1. The actual proportion for the first digit 2 was approximately equal to the common logarithm of 3/2 and so on through the digits ending with the actual proportion for the first digit 9 approximating the common logarithm of 10/9.

Benford then noted that that the observed probabilities related closely to "events" than to the number system itself. He noted that some of the best fits to the logarithmic pattern (of the digits) was for data in which the numbers had no relationship to each other, such as the numbers from newspaper articles. He then linked the logarithmic pattern of the digits to a geometric progression (or geometric sequence) as follows:

> "In natural events and in events of which man considers himself the originator there are plenty of examples of geometric or logarithmic progressions" (Benford, 1938, p.562).

> ... One is tempted to think that the 1, 2, 3... scale is not the natural scale; but that, invoking the base e of the natural logarithms, Nature Counts, e0, ex, e2x, e3x... and builds and functions accordingly" (Benford 1938, p.563).

FIGURE 2.1

AN EXAMPLE OF A GEOMETRIC SEQUENCE

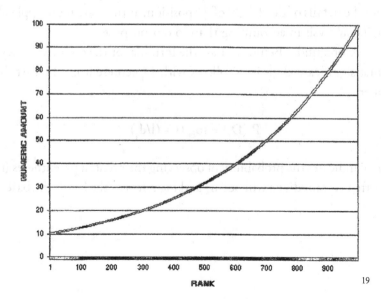

A geometric sequence is a sequence in which each successive term is the previous term multiplied by a common ratio. An example of such a sequence is shown in Figure 2.1 above. The usual mathematical representation for such a sequence is given by:

$$Sn = arn\text{-}1$$

Where *a* is the first term in the sequence, *r* is the common ration, and *n* denotes the nth term. In this example, *a* equals 10, r (the common ration) equals 1.002305, and there are 1,000 terms in the sequence.[20]

Using the assumption that the ordered (rank from smallest to largest) records form a geometric sequence, Benford then derived the expected frequencies of the digits for tabulated "natural" data. The expected (as calculated) frequencies for <u>first digits only</u> are shown again here in Table 1.

Table 1. Theoretical logarithmic law (the number zero cannot be the first significant digit).

First digit	1	2	3	4	5	6	7	8	9
Frequency %	*30.1*	*17.6*	*12.5*	*9.7*	*7.9*	*6.7*	*5.8*	*5.1*	*4.6*

<u>These frequencies have now become known as Benford's Law.</u> Since we are only concerned with the first significant number position, we will not go into the details of the 2nd, 3rd of 4th position, as these are more applicable to digital analysis in accounting than to our purpose.

Therefore, under Benford's Law the formula for the digit frequency of the first significant digit is as follows with D_1 representing the first digit number:

$$\mathbf{P\ (D_1) = log\ (1 + (1/d_1)}$$

where P indicates the probability of observing the event in parentheses (i.e., how often certain digits will occur) and log refers to the log to the base 10.

Observations

Does your house address start with the digit 1? According Benford's Law, about 1/3 of house numbers has "1" as their first digit. The same holds true for many other (data set) areas that have almost nothing in common: the Dow Jones index history, size of files stored on a PC, the length of the world's rivers, the numbers in newspapers' front page headlines, death rate, half-lives of radioisotopes, prime numbers and many, many more. In other words, just about any group of data obtained by using measurements satisfies the law.

On the other hand, data sets that are completely arbitrary and contain artificial floors or ceilings or other constraints do not follow Benford's Law. Examples would be lottery numbers, telephone numbers, gas prices, weights, and heights of a random group of people—numbers not associated with measurements.

This law tells how often each number (from 1 to 9) appears as the first significant digit in a very diverse range of data sets. The number 1 consistently appearing about 1/3 of the time, number 2 appears with a frequency of 17.6%, number 3 at 12.5%, on down to number 9 at 4.6%. Again, in mathematical terms, this logarithmic law is written as **F (d) = log [1 + (1/d)]**, where F is the frequency and d is the digit in question. (Note: this formula is the same as the one above, with slightly different nomenclature.)

If this sounds somewhat strange to you, scientists Jesus Torres, Sonsoles Fernandez, Antonio Gamero, and Antonio Sola from the Universidad de Cordoba in Spain also call the feature surprising. The scientists published a letter in the European Journal of Physics in 2007 called "How do numbers begin?" After giving a short historical review of the law, they list some well-known useful applications and explain that <u>no one has been able to provide an underlying reason for the consistent frequencies.</u>

"The Benford law has been an intriguing question for me for years, ever since I read about it," Torres, who specializes in plasma physics, told *PhysOrg.com*. "I have used it as a surprising example at statistical physics classes to arouse the curiosity of my pupils."

As Torres and his colleagues explain, scientists in the decades following Benford performed numerous studies, but discovered little more about the law other than racking up a wide variety of examples. They discovered that many numerical distributions appeared fulfilling Benford's Law. Practically any group of data obtained carrying out "measurement" satisfied the law, provided the numbers were not arbitrarily assigned and without restriction (telephone numbers, identity cards, area codes or passport numbers, dates, etc.), and are neither random uniform nor normal distributions (lottery, weight and/or height of adult people, etc.). *The astonishing thing was the variety of different data obeying the law. Benford's law was revealed to be a statistical law and therefore the greater the number of elements in a numerical group, the better it would fit to this law.*[21] (Emphasis added)

However, scientists did discover a few curiosities. For one, when investigating second significant digits of data sets, the law still held, but with less importance. Similarly, for the third and fourth digits, the appearance of the numbers started becoming equal, leveling out at a uniform 10% for the fifth digit. However, a second discovery attracted even more interest from scientists:

Another surprising discovery was that although some groups of data do not fulfil the law, their union in a unique set can follow Benford's law, whenever they are not related to each other and have a statistically high number of elements.

"In 1961, Pinkham discovered the first general relevant result, demonstrating that Benford's law is scale invariant and is also the only law referring to digits which can have this scale invariance," the scientists wrote in their letter. "That is to say, as the length of the rivers of the world in kilometers fulfill Benford's law, it is certain that these same data expressed in miles, light years, and microns or in any other length units will also fulfill it." Scientific interest in the law increased as a consequence of this very attractive unicity theorem.[22]

Tores et al. also explain that in the last years of the 20th century, some important theoretical advances have been proven (base invariance, unity, etc.), mainly by Ted Hill and other mathematicians. The scientists also explain that there is no assumed or known criterion that tells when a group of data should or should not obey the law. As Professor Hill said, *"the final chapter of this history has not been written yet."*(Emphasis added)

"Nowadays there are many theoretical results about the law, but some points remain in darkness," said Torres. *"Why do some numerical sets, like universal physical constants, follow the law so well? We need to know not only mathematical reasons for the law, but also how to characterize this set of experimental data. For example, what are their points of contact? Where do they come from? Apparently, they are independent."* Emphasis added.

"I hope the general necessary and sufficient conditions will be discovered in the future as many people are interested in the law, especially economists; but I also know it could be not possible ever," he added, mentioning Gödel.[23]

Nevertheless, scientists have been using the law for many practical applications. For example, because a year's accounting data of a company should fulfill the law, economists can detect falsified data, which is very hard to manipulate to follow the law. (Interestingly, scientists found that numbers 5 and 6, rather than 1, are the most prevalent, suggesting that forgers try to "hide" data in the middle.)

Benford's law has also been recently applied to electoral fraud in order to detect voting anomalies. Scientists found that the 2004 US presidential election showed anomalies in the state of Florida, as well as fraud in Venezuela in 2004 and Mexico in 2006.

"The story about how it was discovered—twice—from dirty pages... it is almost incredible," said Torres. "Benford's law has undeniable applications, and this useful asset was not clear when the law was discovered. It seemed to be only a math curiosity. For me, this is an example of how simplicity can be unexpectedly marvelous."

CHAPTER 3

Benford's Law: The Answer
How does this Law Work?

"A mathematician, like a painter or a poet, is a maker of patterns. If his patterns are more permanent that theirs, it is because they are made with ideas."

G. H. Hardy, A Mathematician's Apology (Cambridge University Press, 1940)

"Just as there are hidden patterns in the chaos we know as data, as discovered by physicist Frank Benford in the 1930s, there are also hidden patterns in the elemental (atomic level) structure of nature."

...the authors

(**Note to reader: The majority of this chapter on Benford's law is taken from my first book, *The Organized Universe*, and is presented in the context of critiquing natural selection as part of Darwin's theory of evolution; nevertheless, these references to evolution in no way affect the explanation or application of the law as demonstrated in this book.**)

In this pioneering journey, we will discover there are indeed hidden patterns (or order) in what appears to be the seeming chaos of matter in the Universe and Planet Earth. We will also discover the cosmic interconnection of those patterns as defined by Benford's Law. We will reveal the divinely designed connection between the hidden pattern of matter in all of God's creation, both in the natural world and in all living organisms including man, and in the divinely inspired Word of God as found in the scriptures of the Old and New Testaments of the Christian Bible (KJV).

Before this unfolds, a further review and discussion is warranted to fully understand the importance of this remarkable discovery called Benford's Law.

As discussed briefly in the previous chapter, Benford's Law, also called the "the law of first digits", states that in lists of tabulated data or numbers from both natural and real-life sources, the leading significant digit 1 occurs much more often than the digits 2 through 9 (namely about 30+% of the time). Furthermore, the larger the digit, the less likely it is to occur as the leading digit of a number. (See Table 1 in the previous chapter.) This applies to figures related to the natural world or those of social significance. Empirical evidence of Benford's Law in numerical data has appeared in a wide variety of contexts including physical and mathematical constants, numbers taken from electricity bills, newspaper articles, street addresses, stock prices, almanacs, population numbers, death rates, areas or lengths of rivers and many areas of accounting and demographic data. More recently, diverse uses have been found in the detection of fraud in medical tests, identifying families of plankton, creating better design for computer hard drives and mathematical modeling. This discovery of a skewed distribution of natural numbers seems on the surface to be counterintuitive, but as you will see, the law never fails to work.

To expand on an earlier statement, this law does not apply to the following distribution types: (1) lottery numbers distribution, (2) standard bell curve distribution or, (3) calculation of atomic weights (4) series of numbers generated by some mathematical functions such as the square root $\sqrt{x}$, the inverse $1/x$ or the square x^2.

However, based on the groundbreaking work by Hill, amazingly, a random sampling from these same distributions will yield digital frequencies close to the Law of First Digits. These new samples from random distributions become log distributions following the Law of First Digits. (Emphasis added)

Benford's paper entitled "The Law of Anomalous Numbers" mentioned above challenged common beliefs about numbers describing random or "natural" phenomena. It would intuitively seem that the digits in these numbers would have an equal probability of occurring. For example, it would seem that each digit from "1" to "9" would have an equal chance of being the first digit in a number. Not so, according to Frank Benford. When he analyzed the digit frequencies from a wide range of natural phenomena, he found that, in every instance, the frequencies approximated those found in Table 1.

Benford formulated the expected frequencies of digits in tabulated data by assuming that they followed a logarithmic distribution. This theoretical frequency, [P (d) = log (1+1/d where P equals the probability or frequency and d equals any first digit 1-9)], has become known as Benford's Law. We will perform a detailed analysis of this formula later in the chapter.

As mentioned earlier, Simon Newcomb also described this phenomenon and even gave the same logarithmic formula for it in 1881. However, it was Benford's rediscovery and testing that placed his name on the law. Strangely enough, the fact that the law was named after Benford and not Simon Newcomb is known as "Stigler's law of eponymy" in which Stigler, a University of Chicago statistics professor, states: "No scientific discovery is named after it original discoverer." Even stranger still, Stigler named the sociologist Robert K. Merton as the discoverer of "Stigler's law" thus, consciously making "Stigler's law" exemplify itself.

In 1996, Ted Hill, noted for his earlier work on Benford's Law, provided the most significant mathematical advance and proof in Benford's theory since Pinkham (1961) by proving the result about mixed distributions. He showed that:

> If distributions are selected at random (in any "unbiased" way), and random samples are then taken from each of these distributions, the significant digits of the resulting collection will converge to the logarithmic (Benford) distribution. This helps explain why the significant digit phenomenon appears in many empirical contexts, and helps explain its recent application to computer design, mathematical modeling, and detection of fraud in account data.[24]

Because of Hill's extensive proof on the underlying theorems of Benford's Law, today this Law is firmly rooted in the modern mathematical theory of probability with its important applications to society. Moreover, the law is now considered one of the natural laws of the universe and science therefore placing it in the lofty company of Newton's Law of Gravitation, the speed of light and other fundamental physical constants.

For many years, only a few people consisting of mathematicians and the Benford family knew this little secret. In the 1990s, the accountant Mark J. Nigrini first advocated the use of Benford's Law as a test for fraud and of data integrity. He has since gone on to become the first person to utilize Benford's Law in detecting financial and accounting fraud. He is a former Southern Methodist University professor and now professor at The College of New Jersey where he teaches forensic accounting courses and has written two books on the subject. His research involves advanced theoretical work on Benford's Law and the legal process surrounding fraud detection and convictions.[25]

Everyday numbers obey a law so unexpected it is hard to believe!

It is a law so unexpected that at first many people simply refuse to believe it can be true. Indeed, only in the past few years has a solid mathematical explanation of its existence emerged. Nevertheless, after years of being regarded as a mathematical curiosity, Benford's law now has the attention of everyone from tax inspectors to computer designers— all of whom think it could help them solve some tricky problems with astonishing ease. The US Institute of Internal Auditors has held training courses on how to apply Benford's law in fraud investigations, hailing it as the biggest advance in the field in years.

Like Newcomb, Benford did not have any good explanation for the existence of the law. Even so, the sheer wealth of evidence he provided to demonstrate its reality and ubiquity has led to his name being linked with the law ever since.

It was nearly a quarter of a century before anyone came up with a plausible answer to the central question: why on earth should the law apply to so many different sources of numbers? The first big step came in 1961 with some neat lateral thinking by Roger Pinkham, a mathematician then at Rutgers University in New Brunswick, New Jersey. Just suppose, said Pinkham, there really is a universal law governing the digits of numbers that describe such diverse natural phenomena such as the drainage areas of rivers and the properties of chemicals. Then any such law must work regardless of what units are used. Even the inhabitants of the Planet Zob, who measure area in grondekis, must find exactly the same distribution of digits in drainage areas as we do, using hectares. But how is this possible, if there are 87.331 hectares to the grondeki?

The answer, said Pinkham, lies in ensuring that the distribution of digits is unaffected by changes of units. Suppose you know the drainage area in hectares for a million different rivers. Translating each of these values into grondekis will change the individual numbers, certainly. Overall, the distribution of numbers would still have the same pattern as before. This is a property known as "scale invariance".

Pinkham showed mathematically that Benford's law is indeed scale-invariant. Crucially, however, he also showed that Benford's law is the only way to distribute digits that have this property. In other words, any "law" of digit frequency with pretensions of universality has no choice but to be Benford's law.

Pinkham's work gave a major boost to the credibility of the law, and prompted others to start taking it seriously and thinking up possible applications. But a key question remained: just what kinds of numbers could be expected to follow Benford's law? Two rules of thumb quickly emerged. For a start, the sample of numbers should be big enough to give the predicted proportions a chance to assert themselves. Second, the numbers should be free of artificial limits and allowed to take any value they please. It is clearly pointless expecting, say, the prices of 10 different types of beer to conform to Benford's law. Not only is the sample too small, but, more importantly, the prices are forced to stay within a fixed, narrow range by market forces.

[Author's note: As it applies to Benford's Law, it is argued by mathematicians and statisticians that only large data sets (also known as a Benford set in this context), having at least a population of 1000, is required to show conformity to the Law of First Digits.[26] However, as will be shown in this chapter, many

data sets of far less that 1000 (e.g., physical constants of the universe and elements of seawater) will show almost perfect conformity to Benford. This, you will see, is an astounding revelation, as this close of "goodness of fit" is statistically impossible according to experts. This also underscores that fact that Benford and others after him did not have any good explanation for the existence of the law.]

Random numbers

As mentioned earlier, truly random numbers will not conform to Benford's law either: the proportions of leading digits in such numbers are, by definition, equal. Benford's Law applies to numbers occupying the middle ground.

Below is a short discussion and illustration of random numbers.

Random Chance Defined

As opposed to the term "random chance" as used in the natural selection process of Darwinian Evolution, the word "random" as used in statistics or mathematics means that each item has an equal chance of being selected. Thus, there is a pre-determined collective order. For example, if the natural numbers 1 through 9 were randomly selected, the number of ones would be selected in the same proportion or percentage as any other natural number according to a precise collective mathematical formula, i.e.

$$P = \frac{1}{n + (9-n)} \text{ (x 100 for percent)}$$

P – Proportion or Probability of Appearance

n – natural number

Example 1

n = 1

$$P = \frac{1}{1 + 8} = \frac{1}{9} = .1111 = 11.11\%$$

Example 2

n = 6

$$P = \frac{1}{6 + 3} = \frac{1}{9} = .1111 = 11.11\%$$

	1	2	3	4	5	6	7	8	9
Actual Count	28	21	14	3	14	0	7	11	18	14
Theoretical Count		11	11	11	11	11	11	11	11	11
Actual Count	207	14	12	12	8	12	9	15	9	9

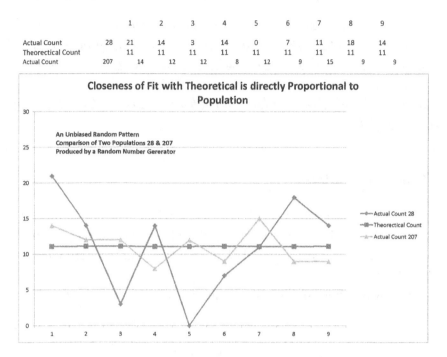

Closeness of Fit with Theoretical is directly Proportional to Population

An Unbiased Random Pattern
Comparison of Two Populations 28 & 207
Produced by a Random Number Gererator

—◆—Actual Count 28
—■—Theorectical Count
—▲—Actual Count 207

As you can see, the larger the population of truly random numbers, the closer the fit to the theoretical of just over 11%. What does this say about small population counts in nature that conform to Benford's law in a better than perfect? Most would assume this either impossible or a trick. These small population counts are demonstrated in some of the graphs later in this chapter.

Precisely what all of this means remained a mystery until 1995 when mathematician Theodore Hill, formerly of Georgia Institute of Technology in Atlanta, uncovered what appears to be the true origin of Benford's Law. It comes, he realized, from the various ways that different kinds of measurements tend to spread themselves. Ultimately, everything we can measure in the Universe is the outcome of some process or other: the random jolts of atoms, say, or the exigencies of genetics. Mathematicians have long known that the spread of values for each of these follows some basic mathematical rule. <u>So it appears that Benford's Law is the universal link and mathematical rule for everything measureable in the universe.</u> The heights of bank managers, for example, follow the bell-shaped Gaussian curve; daily temperatures rise and fall in a wave-like pattern, while the strength and frequency of earthquakes are linked by a logarithmic law.

Now imagine grabbing random handfuls of data from a hotchpotch of such distributions. Hill proved that as you grab ever more of such numbers, the digits of these numbers will conform ever closer to a single specific law is a kind of ultimate distribution, the "Distribution of Distributions". Moreover, he showed *"that its mathematical form is… Benford's law."* Emphasis added.

Hill's theorem, published in 1996, seems finally to explain the astonishing ubiquity of Benford's law. For while numbers describing some phenomena are under the control of a single distribution such as the bell curve, many more—describing everything from census data to stock market prices—are dictated by a random mix of all kinds of distributions. If Hill's theorem is correct, this means that the digits of these data should follow Benford's law. In addition, as Benford's own monumental study and many others have shown, they really do. Nevertheless, as Hill states, "nobody knows how fast you can get to Benford's Law—how many numbers need to be in a list before the digits will show a Benford distribution?"

<u>We show that, contrary to Hill and others, a population (not sample) as small as 82 in a natural application will conform to Benford</u>. This unique digital pattern of Benford's law is woven throughout everything we know and see in the natural world and will unquestionably overturn at least one strongly established paradigm of science—namely that of Darwin's Theory of Evolution and its Post Darwinian postulates. (See my first book, *The Organized Universe.)*

Naysayers

As in any new field of discovery or application, there will be those who voice objections, valid or otherwise. The most common critical objections against the Law of First Digits as being a legitimate natural law of science can be stated in several ways as follows:

1. The Law is merely the result of our way of writing numbers.
2. The Law is just a built in characteristic of our number system.

3. The digit one (1) is first, thus it will appear more frequently than the others....period.

However, it is interesting to note that these critics are not denying that the first digit natural numbers 1- 9 appear at the following frequency in nature:

Table 2

1 30.1%	6 6.7%
2 17.6%	7 5.8%
3 12.5%	8 5.1%
4 9.7%	9 4.6%
5 7.9%	

If their objections were correct, then the same frequencies or percentages would be true for the second digits of numbers when we exclude all single digit numbers. The second digits of numbers appear as zero through nine or ten total digits instead of nine total digits for the first digit numbers of the natural numbers one through nine.

Mark Nigrini sees Hill's theorem as a crucial breakthrough: "It... helps explain why the significant digit phenomenon appears in so many contexts."

It has also helped Nigrini to convince others that Benford's law is much more than just a bit of mathematical frivolity. Over the past few years, Nigrini has become the driving force behind a far from frivolous use of the law: financial fraud detection.

In a groundbreaking doctoral thesis published in 1992, Nigrini showed that many key features of accounts, from sales figures to expenses claims, follow Benford's law, and that deviations from the law can be quickly detected using standard statistical tests. Nigrini calls the fraud busting technique "digital analysis" and its successes are starting to attract interest in the corporate world and beyond.

Some of the earliest cases—including the sharp practices of Alex's storekeeping brother-in-law—emerged from student projects set up by Nigrini. Soon he was using digital analysis to unmask much bigger frauds. One recent case involved an American leisure and travel company with a nationwide chain of motels. Using digital analysis, the company's audit director discovered something odd about the claims being made by the supervisor of the company's healthcare department. "The first two digits of the healthcare payments were checked for conformity to Benford's law, and this revealed a spike in numbers beginning with the digits 65," says Nigrini. "An audit showed 13 fraudulent checks for between $6500 and $6599...related to fraudulent heart surgery claims processed by the supervisor, with the check ending up in her hands."

Benford's law had exposed the supervisor despite her best efforts to make the claims look plausible. "She carefully chose to make claims for employees at motels with a higher than normal number of older employees," says Nigrini. "The analysis also uncovered other fraudulent claims worth around $1 million in total."

Not surprisingly, big businesses and central governments are now also starting to take Benford's law seriously. "Digital analysis is being used by listed companies, large private companies, professional firms and government agencies in the US and Europe and by one of the world's largest audit firms, says Nigrini.

Warning Signs

The technique is also attracting interest from those hunting for other kinds of fraud. At the International Institute for Drug Development in Brussels, Mark Buyse and his colleagues believe Benford's law could reveal suspicious data in clinical trials, while a number of university researchers have contacted Nigrini to find out if digital analysis could help reveal fraud in laboratory notebooks.

Inevitably, the increasing use of digital analysis will lead to greater awareness of its power by fraudsters. But according to Nigrini, that knowledge won't do them much good— apart from warning them off: "The problem for fraudsters is that they have no idea what the whole picture looks like until all the data are in, says Nigrini." Frauds usually involve just a part of a data set, but the fraudsters do not know how that set will be analyzed: by quarter, say, or department, or by region. Ensuring the fraud always complies with Benford's Law is going to be tough, and most fraudsters aren't rocket scientists."

In any case, says Nigrini, there is more to Benford's law than tracking down fraudsters. Take the data explosion that threatens to overwhelm data storage technology. Mathematician Peter Schatte at the Bergakademie Technical University, Freiberg, has come up with rules that optimize computer data storage, by allocating disk space according to the proportions dictated by Benford's law.

Ted Hill thinks that the ubiquity of Benford's law could also prove useful to those such as Treasury forecasters and demographers who need a simple "reality check" for their mathematical models. "Nigrini showed recently that the populations of the 3,000-plus counties in the US are very close to Benford's law," says Hill. "That suggests it could be a test for models which predict future populations—if the figures predicted are not close to Benford, then rethink the model."

Both Nigrini and Hill stress that Benford's law is not a panacea for fraud busters or the world's data crunching ills. Deviations from the law's predictions can be caused by nothing more nefarious than rounding numbers up or down, for example. And both accept that there is plenty of scope for making a hash of applying it to real-life situations: "Every mathematical theorem or statistical test can be misused—that does not worry me," says Hill.

But they share a sense that there are some really clever uses of Benford's law still waiting to be dreamt up. Says Hill: "For me the law is a prime example of a mathematical idea which is a surprise to everyone—even the experts."

As used today, Benford's Law or the Law of First Digits is a powerful, yet simple mathematical tool for pointing suspicion at frauds, embezzlers, tax evaders, sloppy accountants, and even computer bugs. The income tax agencies of several nations and states, including California, are using detection software based on Benford's Law, as are a score of large companies and accounting businesses. The IRS, the U.S. Institute of Internal Auditors and the International Institute for Drug Development in Brussels are all working on ways to use the Law.

Until this author's unique application of Benford's Law, as detailed in *The Organized Universe*, this natural law of science was used almost exclusively in the above described accounting/detection area as well as some applications in signal processing and hydrology.

A few more details in this short history and background of Benford's Law will give you a better picture of its evolvement and how, today, it is recognized as a true natural law of science, one with the same theoretical weight as Newton's law of gravity or other fundamental physical constants of the universe. It has come a long way from just a mathematical curiosity as late as the 1950s. We will also examine the Law's simple mathematical statement, which explains why the leading digit 1 is more common than the other digits in every natural data set environment.

Remember that we said the discovery of this fact goes back to 1881, when the American astronomer Simon Newcomb noticed that the first pages of logarithm books the ones containing numbers that started with 1 were much more worn than the other pages. We also said that Benford's Law is named for the late Dr. Frank Benford, who also noticed that pages of logarithms corresponding to numbers starting with the numeral 1 were much dirtier and more worn than other pages of the table, just as Newcomb had. This was a key element in Dr. Benford's discovery.

(For those of you who may have forgotten or never used logarithms, a logarithm is simply an exponent. Any number can be expressed as a fractional exponent, the logarithm of some base number, such as 10. John Napier discovered logarithms in 1614 and Joost Burgi published the First Table of Logarithms in 1620. Published tables permit users to look up logarithms corresponding to numbers, or numbers corresponding to logarithms. This was the preferred method of adding, subtracting or dividing large numbers in lieu of using laborious long hand calculations prior to the advent of calculators and computers.)

What are the effects of Benford's Law on number sequences? Intuitively, most people assume that in a string of numbers sampled randomly from some body of data derived from nature or in every day natural living events, the first nonzero digit could be any number from 1 through 9. All nine numbers would be regarded as equally probable. As you have probably guessed by now, this is not the case, even with random samples of data sets.

As the story goes, Professor Hill asks his mathematics students at the Georgia Institute of Technology to go home and either flip a coin 200 times and record the results, or merely pretend to flip a coin and fake

200 results. The following day he quickly reviews their homework and to their amazement, Dr. Hill easily identifies nearly all those who faked their tosses. Before you go and attempt to solve this trick by doing your own coin toss, know that the quick answer and reason is that in a random chance coin toss (assuming no toss control or rhythm), there will normally be a consistent string of 6 or 7 heads or tails in the overall distribution. So spotting any results absent this pattern is relatively easy.

Then the question arose: if a distribution of first digits exits, should it be scale invariant? As we stated earlier, Roger Pinkham, a mathematician then at Rutgers University, proved this hypothesis in 1961. He demonstrated data sets conforming to Benford's Law should have the same distribution regardless of the units of measurements used: whether feet or meters, dollars or pesos, pounds or kilograms, gallons or liters, or anything else. For example, there are three feet in a yard, so the probability that the first digit of a length (e.g. in yards) is 1 must be the same as the probability that the first digit of a length (e.g. in feet) starts 3, 4, or 5. Applying this to all possible measurement scales gives a logarithmic distribution, and combined with the fact that $\log_{10} (1) = 0$ and $\log_{10} (10) = 1$ gives Benford's law. That is, if there is a distribution of first digits, it must apply to a set of data regardless of what measuring units are used, and the only distribution of first digits that fits that is the Benford Law.

As also stated earlier, the consensus among statisticians and mathematicians regarding the size of a data set used for analysis is that there should be a reasonably large number of records. Nigrini asserts that Benford's Law is a limiting distribution, and underlying calculus *assumes* that we have reasonably large numbers. He further states that he has "found that conformity to Benford's Law requires that we have a large data table with numbers that have at least four digits".

Our research has shown this to be only half true. While we agree that there should be at least four digits (or 4th order magnitude) in the numbers, we demur as to the required large data set of a least 1000 records[27]. As you will see in a few pages, we have demonstrated that *even small populations (not just samples) of less than 100 in applications to varied natural phenomena not only conform to Benford but do so in a better than perfect fit under the conformity tests.* This becomes a powerful and revealing statement in the light of its supposed impossibility.

So even using such small population records, there are enough numbers in the sample data set to conform to Benford such that the first digit of the sequence is more likely to be 1 than any other number. Therefore, by extension, mathematicians have found that the larger and more varied the sampling of numbers from different data sets the more closely the distribution of numbers approaches what Benford's Law predicted. In addition, the greater the number of digits (accuracy) in the numbers, the greater the conformity even in the smaller data sets.

To expand our appreciation of the universality and interconnectedness of Benford's law, consider the "coincidence" of nature's preferences in numbers and sequences that have long fascinated mathematicians. The so-called Golden Mean—roughly equal to 1.62 and supposedly giving the most aesthetically pleasing dimensions for rectangles—has been found lurking in all kinds of unexpected places from seashells to knots. Likewise, the Fibonacci sequence—1, 1, 2, 3, 5, 8, 13, 21 and so on, every figure being the sum of its two predecessors—crops up everywhere in nature from the arrangement of leaves on plants to the pattern on pineapple skins. Benford's Law appears to be another fundamental feature of the mathematical universe, with the proportion of numbers starting with the digit D given by $\log_{10}$ of $(1 + 1/D)$. In other words around 100 x $\log_2$ (30%) of such numbers will begin with "1"; 100 x $\log_{1.5}$ (17.6%) with "2"; down to 100 x $\log_{1.11}$ (4.6%) with "9".

> *I see a certain order in the universe and math is one way of making it visible.*
>
> ### May Sarton (1925 – 1995)

Although not within the scope of this book, it should be stated that the mathematics of Benford's law goes even further, predicting the proportion of digits in the rest of the numbers as well. For example, the law predicts that "0" is the most likely second digit—accounting for around 12 % of all second digits—while 9 is the least likely, at 8.5%. Benford's law thus suggests that the most common nonrandom numbers are those starting with "10...", which should be almost 10 times more abundant than the least likely, which would be those starting with "99...". As one might expect, Benford's law predicts that the relative proportions of 1, 2, 3 and so on, making up latter digits of numbers, become progressively more even, tending towards precisely 10 percent of the least significant digit of every large number. *In a nice little twist, it turns out that the Fibonacci sequence, the Golden Mean and Benford's law are all linked. The ratio of successive terms in a Fibonacci sequence tend toward the golden mean, while the digits of all the numbers making up the Fibonacci sequence tend to conform to Benford's law.*[28]

> *Our task is to find an algorithm, a natural law that leads to the origin of information.*
>
> *-Manfred Eigen*[29]

To date, the significance of the Benford's Law was previously greatly underestimated and not fully realized, as prophesied in Hill's earlier statement. The author has conducted considerable research into applications of the Law into areas previously unknown or even considered. This research, as applied to both physical measurements of the universe and true-life happenings, occurrences and events as described in *The Organized Universe* with its conclusive proof, offers the following observations and results:

- It measures conformity *and nonconformity* to true-life happenings, occurrences and events and true physical arrangements of chemical matter. In other words, it *measures whether something is natural or unnatural*. A question to ponder is, by extension, does this imply truth or non-truth? Further research into this subject may yield surprising results.
- It conforms to true natural measurements of fundamental physical constants of the universe and planet earth and vice versa. These are unalterable, infallible known laws of the universe such as Newton's gravitational constant, the speed of light in a vacuum, etc.
- It regulates and dictates the structure of other true natural Laws of Science thus it could be considered as the "Law of Laws".
- It is scale and base invariant: no matter what unit of measurement or base number system you use, the initial unit (first significant digit 1) of measurement will occur most frequently as proscribed by the law.
- Benford's Law is a built in characteristic of our number system.

To reiterate, the Law of First Digits states that certain numbers show up more frequently than others do. In order to demonstrate this, the size of the following numbers in graphic form denotes the frequency that the number may appear in nature in different environments.

In the Chaotic Array of Numbers environment, as shown below), each number may appear in any amount of frequency that cannot be predicted or predetermined.

Chaotic Array

$$1 2_3 4 5_6 7 8 9$$

In the Random Pattern (Un*biased*) environment, each number would appear in an equal amount of frequency.

Random Pattern (Unbiased)

$$123456789$$

However, under the Law of First Digits, each number would appear in the recurring frequency that must conform to a precise mathematical formula as derived from Benford's Law. Therefore, under the Law of First Digits (First Order), the law of natural numbers under Benford's Law will look like this (descending relative proportions):

1 2 3 4 5 6 7 8 9

Are you beginning to see a pattern now?

In our world of numbers, there are 9 natural numbers in our number system with a base of ten 10 that we normally use in everyday life. (Just as an aside, it is a fascinating study to trace the origins of our number system from the early Hindus and eventually through the Arabs of the Middle East.[30])

Back to our everyday natural numbers:

1, 2, 3, 4, 5, 6, 7, 8, 9

A number can be composed of one or more of the natural number digits and which may contain a zero (0) to fill the space in any position before or after the first significant digit.

Consider the number **5,608.**

> The first digit is **5**
> The second digit is **6**
> The third digit is **0** (for our purposes, it is for space only; it is significant, however, when analyzing the first 2 digits of a number.)
> The fourth digit is **8**
> Alternatively, consider the following decimal number:
> **.0035498**

Here the first significant digit is 3 as we ignore the decimal point and the number "0" as The Law of First Digits only considers the first significant digit or other similarly positioned natural numbers 1 through 9.

Criteria That Allows Closer Conformity to the Law of First Digits

Although Benford's Law or the Law of First Digits begins the author's proof, let us further narrow the definition to create an even tighter conformity to the Law. The following allows for further quantifying a closer fit definition:

1. Longer period (time)
2. More Diversity of data, i.e. from various nonrelated natural tabulated data sets.
3. Larger data sets of digits *(although we will demonstrate better than perfect conformity using several small data sets.)*
4. Elimination of duplications and repetitions
5. Values that have no maximums or minimums
6. Elimination of assigned or contrived numbers, such as street addresses, social security numbers, area codes etc.
7. Naturally occurring sets of data.
8. Use of authentic or real data, not contrived or fabricated data.
9. Elimination of fabricated or invented numbers such as computer generated data

We have previously defined Benford's law as a Natural Law of Science. In order for such a Natural Law to be valid, it must pass at least the first three (3) defined invariants of the seven invariants listed in the following test.

Seven (7) Invariants of Natural Laws

1. <u>Scale Invariant</u> – data can be measured or expressed in dollars or pesos, feet or meters, pounds or kilograms, gallons or liters, square miles or square kilometers, etc.
2. <u>Number Base Invariant</u> – any number system base can be used, i.e., 2,5,6,10,20, etc.
3. <u>Time Invariant</u> – does not depend on any specific time period, i.e., 2700 B.C., 1900 A.D., or 2003 A.D., etc.

4. <u>Category or Classification Invariant</u> – does not depend on the matter or items that are measured, i.e., black or white, square or cube, large or small, liquid or solid, wet or dry, etc.

5. <u>Combination Invariant</u> – categories or groups can be combined such as apples or oranges, cats and dogs, men and women, cars and trucks, etc., in the measurement.

6. <u>Relationship Invariant</u> – does not depend on relationships, i.e., married or single, relative or stranger, citizen or alien, friend or enemy, private or public, etc., in measurement.

7. <u>Conversion Factor Invariant</u> – can be multiplied or divided by a certain numerical factor or constant without adversely affecting the distribution.

To our great surprise, The Law of First Digits passed not only the first three (3) tests but passed on all seven (7) of the Invariant's Test thus solidifying the claim that it is a true Law of Nature.

Under the Law of First Digits, the individual numbers or entries have the freedom to be any digit one (1) thru nine (9). However, collectively the individual numbers or entries must conform to the Law of First Digits—a natural law of science that reflects the organized elemental structure of Planet Earth and the Universe.

Let us now look at "The Formula"

The precise formula for the mathematical order that follows a universal scientific law of nature known as the Law of First Digits is:

$$P = \log_{10} (1 + 1/n)$$

Where p = proportion or probability and n = any natural number 1 through 9. For example, if you want to calculate the proportion or percentage of the first digit 3 as it appears in measurements of the Universe and Planet Earth, first make n = 3. Then

$$P = \log_{10} (1+1/3)$$

or

$$P = \log_{10} (1.3333)$$

Using your calculator or computer, find the log of 1.3333 (log 1.333 =)

$$P = \log_{10} (1.3333) = .1249 \text{ (Rounded Off)}$$

or

$$.1249 \times 100 = 12.49\%$$

Therefore, the first digit "3" appears 12.49% in the natural data of the Universe and on Planet Earth.

First Digit Orders

We have talked about first digits having a First Order, Fourth Order, etc. What does this classification mean? Basically, it refers to the 'magnitude' of a number based on a logarithmic scale. In this case we use the common log of base 10. So, the First Order would be digits 1 through 9; Second Order would be digits 10 through 19, etc. Fourth Order is any number >1,000 as reflected in the following Table.

First Order	→	1	▸|	10
Second Order	→	10	▸|	100
Third Order	→	100	▸|	1,000
Fourth Order	→	1000	▸|	∞

▸| - Up to, but not including

Table 3

The underlying idea of Benford's Law is that the natural numbers, expressed in base 10 (and more or less arbitrary), will be evenly *distributed on a logarithmic scale*. This is shown by the exponents on these constants, and demonstrates that they are uniformly distributed (at least over several orders of magnitude). These orders of magnitude are shown above.

The Law of First Digits is so precise that there are different proportions or percentages for

First Digit	First Order	Second Order	Third Order	Fourth Order
—	1 ▸ 10	10 ▸ 100	100 ▸ 1,000	1,000 ▸
1	.3932	.3179	.3028	.3010
2	.2576	.1793	.1764	.1761
3	.1327	.1243	.1249	.1249
4	.0815	.0948	.0967	.0969
5	.0535	.0763	.0789	.0792
6	.0358	.0637	.0667	.0670
7	.0235	.0544	.0576	.0580
8	.0147	.0474	.0508	.0512
9	.0077	.0419	.0454	.0458

(Rounded off to four decimal places)

different sizes or orders of numbers that are first digits.

For Example:

The First Digit "1" in the natural number "1" (1st Order) appears .3932 x 100= 39.32% of the time in nature. The First Digit "1" in the natural number "1,000" (4th Order) appears .3010 x 100 = 30.10% of the time in nature. A table showing the Frequencies of First Digit Orders is shown above.

Theoretical Proportions or Frequencies

As mentioned, the formula for the Law of First Digits has a logarithmic aspect. As described earlier, the table of logarithms was used by scientists and engineers before we had slide rules, calculators and computers to multiply and divide numbers, but their results are just as accurate.

Referring to Table of Logarithms below, the Logarithm of the number 20 is 1.3010.

Table 3

			Law of First Digits		
Number From Table		Logarithm (minus 1)	Logarithmic Difference Between Numbers	First Digit Proportion (Fourth Order)	First Digit
10		0.000			
20		0.3010	.3010- .0000 = .3010	0.3010	1
30		0.4771	.4771- .3010 = .1761	0.1761	2
40		0.6021	.6021- .4771 = .1250	0.1249	3
50		0.6990	.6990- .6021 = .0969	0.0969	4
60		0.7782	.7782- .6990 = .0792	0.0792	5
70		0.8451	.8451- .7782 = .0669	0.0670	6
80		0.9031	.9031- .8451 = .0580	0.0580	7
90		0.9542	.9542- .9031 = .0511	0.0512	8
100		1.000	1.000- .9542 = .0458	0.0458	9

Relationship between the Table of Logarithms and the Law of First Digits

To calculate the fourth order proportion for Digit 1, take the logarithm for 20, 1.3010, and subtract 1 which = .3010. Then, subtracting the previous logarithm of 1.0000 minus 1 from .3010 = .3010 (or 30.10%) which is the proportion for Digit 1 (Fourth Order) involving the Law of First Digits.

It is worth repeating that the Law of First Digit is a valid universal law, such as the Law of Gravity or the speed of light, etc.; accordingly, a rational person would have the same level of confidence in this law as they would in any other valid law of science and nature.

So, how can we use this law and what can it do?

For our purposes, the Law of First Digits measures the following:

1. True Life Happenings, Events and Occurrences and Vice Versa (i.e., false happenings)
2. True Physical Arrangements or Combinations of Chemical Matter or Materials on Earth and throughout the Universe.

One might ask, does the Law of First Digits work independently or does it work in conjunction with other universal laws or principles? The answer is that it is not independent and does work in conjunction with the following known laws (principles), regulating and dictating their structure.

1. Principle of Uniformity or Uniformitarianism

Uniformitarianism is the assumption that the same natural laws and processes that operate in the universe now have always operated in the universe in the past and apply equally everywhere in the universe. It has included the gradualist concept that "the present is the key to the past" and is functioning at the same rates. Uniformitarianism has been a key principle of geology and virtually all fields of science, but naturalism's modern geologists, while accepting that geology has occurred across deep time, no longer hold to a strict gradualism.

Uniformitarianism was formulated by Scottish naturalists in the late 18th century, starting with the work of the geologist James Hutton, which was refined by John Playfair and popularized by Charles Lyell's *Principles of Geology* in 1830. The term *uniformitarianism* was coined by William Whewell, who also coined the term *catastrophism* for the idea that Earth was shaped by a series of sudden, short-lived, violent events.[31] The short version is that "we assume that all natural laws are invariant with time.[32] The Principle of Uniformity says that all natural laws are not dependent on time but are invariant. That is if a law is true today it was true at any time in the past, even when the Universe first formed.

2. Steno Principle of Invariance for Laws of Nature

The Steno Principle of Invariance for Laws of Nature states, in a similar manner, those things that occurred previously operate the same way today.

By using these two principles, we can thus proceed with the mathematical proof.

It is well established that nature has differences or deviations that are still considered normal. If a measurement falls under the standard Bell Curve, which is approximately ±3 standard deviations from a mean or average, it is still normal and natural and fits the norm and vice versa. The closeness of fit to the theoretical mean or average of the Law of First Digits can be determined in the same way by the solving for deviation from the theoretical mean or average. <u>The smaller the standard deviation the better the fit is to the theoretical</u>. The following graph depicts the Standard Deviation variations and scores:

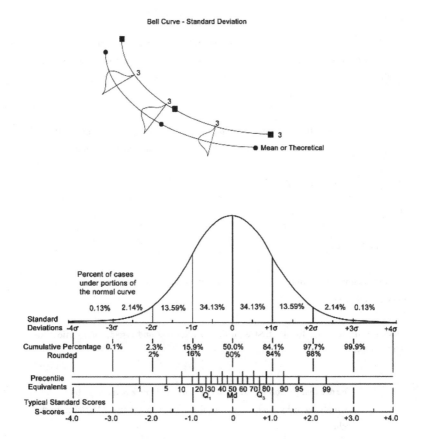

As you can see from the next to last line on the chart, even 3 Standard Deviations from the norm is within 2.14% of the cases on the normal curve. All of the test you will see later in the book will show numbers not only well within the ±3 standard deviations but also, under more stringent tests, will show a "closeness of fit" better than perfect.

As we have shown, all the seemingly unrelated sets of numbers followed the same first digit probability pattern that the worn pages of logarithm tables suggested. In all cases, the number "1" turned up as the first digit about 30 percent of the time more than any other did. Dr. Benford's formula explained this: If absolute certainty is defined as 1 and absolute impossibility as 0, then the probability of any number "d" from 1 through 9 being the first digit is log to the base 10 of (1+1/d). This formula predicts the frequencies of numbers found in many categories of statistics.

The Calculations

Starting with a certain total population of measurements or numbers that have resulted from true real life happenings and events or true physical arrangements of nature, the first digits 1 through 9 are tallied and then independently counted for each of the first digits 1 through 9 derived from those numbers.

First, a ratio of the independent count for each first digit is calculated with the total population of numbers used for the first digits 1 through 9. For example, if the count for the first digit one (1) is X, and the Total Population for the first digits 1 through 9 is N, the ratio would be:

Ratio= X_1/N; if $X_1 = 14$ and N=45, then

The ratio = 14/45

and the decimal proportion is derived by dividing 45 into 14, which equals .3111_to four (4) decimal places.

Likewise, if the count for the first digit nine 9 (X_9) is 2 and N=45, then Ratio= X_9 = 2/45 = .0444

    The decimal proportion .3111 can be converted into a percentage by multiplying it by 100 or moving the decimal point two (2) places to the right.

    Therefore, .3111 becomes 31.11% (Percent)

    and

    .0444 becomes 4.44% (Percent)

Next, the (Z) score or the number of standard deviations from the theoretical count $\ddot{X}$ needs to be determined for each first digit 1 through 9.

First, a theoretical count $\ddot{X}$ needs to be calculated and determined. If the theoretical proportion **P** for the first digit one (1) is .3010, then by multiplying that theoretical proportion of .3010 by the Total Population N of all the First Digits 1 through 9 that is 45, the answer gives the theoretical count $\ddot{X}$. The theoretical property P is obtained from the table of proportions for the Law of First Digits in Table 3 above.

$\ddot{X}_1 = P_1 \times N$ or,

$\ddot{X}_1 = .3010 \times 45 = 13.55$ or 14 (rounded up)

Then the difference or deviation with the Actual Count X can be determined which is:

$X_1 - \ddot{X}_1$; if $X_1 = 10$ and $\ddot{X}_1 = 14$, then $X_1 - \ddot{X}_1 = 4$

The number of Standard Deviations or the (Z) score of a deviation of X $\ddot{X}$ is calculated by:

(Z) Score = X-$\underline{\ddot{X}}$; where ESD is the Estimated Standard Deviation that is derived from the following formula where:

ESD= $\overline{\sqrt{[(1P) \times P] \times N}}$

Where

P = Theoretical Proportion

N = Total Population of First Digits 1- 9

If P =.3010 and N = 45 then,

$ESD_1 = \sqrt{[(1.3010) \times .3010] \times 45}$

$ESD_1 = \sqrt{.2104 \times 45}$ $= \sqrt{9.47}$ $= 3.08$

Again, (Z_1) Score $= \dfrac{X_1 - \ddot{X}_1}{ESD_1}$

Or

$X_1 - \ddot{X}_1 = -4$ and $ESD_1 = 3.08$

Therefore,

$(Z1)$ Score $= \dfrac{-4}{3.08} = 1.30$ Standard Deviations from the theoretical count $\ddot{X}_1$

Each of the other First Digits Actual Counts of X is treated in the same manner.

To test how good a fit the Actual Count X_1 is in comparison to the Theoretical Count $\ddot{X}_1$ taking into consideration the Total Population of all of the First Digits 1-9, which is 45, the application of the Chi Square[i] (pronounced "kigh square) formulas to the (Z) score is considered to be a *very severe test even for large populations.*

In analyzing the Chi Square formula, we sum up everything using the symbol $\sum$.

So, Chi Square=

$$\sum (Z)^2 \text{ or } \sum [(Z_1)^2 + (Z_2)^2 + \ldots\ldots (Z_9)^2]$$

Each (Z) score is then squared and added together.

Another second type of Chi Square test is applied by using the following formula:

Chi Square= $\displaystyle\sum_{1}^{9} \left[\frac{(X - \ddot{X})^2}{X}\right]$

Chi Square = $\displaystyle\sum \left[\frac{(X_1 - \ddot{X}_1)^2}{\ddot{X}_1} + \frac{(X_2 - \ddot{X}_2)^2}{\ddot{X}_1} + \ldots\ldots\ldots\frac{(X_9 - \ddot{X}_9)^2}{\ddot{X}_1}\right]$

Where:

X = Actual Count for each First Digit 1 through 9

$\ddot{X}$ = Theoretical Count for each First Digit 1 through 9

(As an aside, all numbers from each data set in the research were derived by hand and all formula calculations were performed on a hand held Casio fx300W S-VRAM calculator.)

In the Appendixes, the systematic instructions are repeated along with blank forms allowing you to do your own calculations and analysis. As I mentioned in the Introduction, the math shown here is from simple statistical formulae involving standard deviations and the 'goodness of fit' formula of Chi Square, all of which are found in most beginning statistics textbooks and courses. However, for the more mathematically adventurous, I recommend Theodore P. Hills' original research paper entitled, *A Statistical Derivation of the Significant Digit Law*, which contains a detailed description and proof of his ground breaking mathematical theorem confirming the scientific validity of Benford's Law.

I think it is important to reemphasize the significance of this new statistical derivation of Mr. Hill by quoting directing from page 14 of his paper:

> "The stage is now set to give a new statistical limit law (Theorem 3 below) which is a central limit like theorem for significant digits. Roughly speaking, this law says that if probability distributions are selected at random,

and random samples are then taken from each of these distributions in a way so that the overall process is scale (or base) neutral, then the significant digit frequencies of the combined sample will converge to the logarithmic distribution. This theorem helps explain and predict the appearance of the logarithmic distribution in significant digits of tabulated data."

This explains the reason for the law's universality and the present logarithmic nature in all distributions of significant digits of tabulated data—and by extension the reflective order of the makeup of all matter.

Applications to Nature

To more fully understand the relationship of our proof of Benford's law to the natural world, let us first examine an aspect of Darwinian Evolution, which was the subject of the first book, *The Organized Universe (the principles described below demonstrate the universality of Benford's which we will later apply to the Holy Scripture)*; we must first restate some of basic tenants of which all Darwinian Evolutionists agree:

1) That air (devoid of oxygen), water and newly formed rock, inorganic or lifeless material were the only raw materials available on early earth.[33]

2) Absent any outside force, the first living entities must have been fabricated from these primitive resources. This, of course, begs the question of how life was introduced into these primitive resources. Moreover, how could these entities be self-organizing and self-replicating if they originated from such dead matter?

So let's investigate these statements. In stating the obvious, there are three (3) different forms of matter to consider. They are:

I.   Solid
II. Liquid
III. Gaseous (Vapor)

Normally, the discussion concerning matter would begin with the solid category, but because Darwinian Evolution begins with "a warm little pond" or saltwater (Liquid) some 4.0 Billion years ago, this shall be our starting point.

Liquid Matter

There are numerous examples of applications of The Law of First Digits to measurements of matter and life events throughout the Universe and Planet Earth, but the measurements of the quantity of basic elements in seawater is especially significant because Darwin Evolution starts with "Primordial Soup" or seawater.[34]

All of the matter that we see on Earth, including all living creatures and man, and the matter that makes up the stars is composed of elemental particles of protons, neutrons and electrons (plus the mysterious "muon"—the 'overweight electron'). Everything around you is composed of only about 90 different types of atoms: 90 different arrangements of protons, neutrons and electrons. These different *types* of atoms are known as Elements. A full listing of these Elements along with their atomic number, name and symbol can be found in a book titled, *The elements: The New Guide to the Building Blocks of our Universe*[35]

The Elements

This list consists of the known natural elements (92); as of 2012, there are additional elements known as The Transuranium Elements which is any element with an atomic number greater than 92 (the atomic number of uranium). Until the 1930s, scientists supposed that uranium was the heaviest element that could exist. However, advances in the understanding and technology of nuclear physics have led to the artificial creation of transuranium elements in laboratories, nuclear reactors, nuclear explosions and particle accelerators.[36] As an example, Plutonium would be the most recognizable element from this group.

Below is a *Sample Population* (out of a total population of 81) of the Abundance (quantity) of Elements in the Earth's Sea[37] This table gives the estimated abundance of the elements in seawater near the surface (in mg/L).

Element	Amount	First Digit
Ag	4 x 10e5	4
Al	2 x 10e3	2
Ar	4.5 x 10e1	4
As	3.7 x 10e3	3
Au	4 x 10e6	4
B	4.44	4
Ba	1.3 x 10e2	1
Be	5.6 x 10e6	5
Bi	2 x 10e3	2
Br	6.73 x 10e1	6
C	2.8 x 10e1	2
Ca	4.12 x 10e2	4
Cd	1.1 x 10e4	1
Ce	1.2 x 10e5	1
Cl	1.94 x 10e4	1
Co	2 x 10e—5	2
Cr	3 x 10e4	3
Cs	3 x 10e4	3
Cu	2.5 x 10e4	2
Dy	9.1 x 10e7	9
Er	8.7 x 10e7	8

The methodology now is to add up the number of 1's, 2's, 3's, 4's, etc. in the First Digit column and record the total amounts in the Actual Population, the "X" Column, on the upcoming chart (page 89) concerning the Abundance of Elements in the Earth's Sea.

Next, after the calculations are complete, compare the two "closeness of fit" scores (Z) scores[38] and the Chi Square scores[39] with the Interpretation of the Numbers chart below.

Interpretation of the Numbers

Z Standard Deviation

0 to +1	Near Perfect Fit, Statistically Speaking[40]
+1 to +2	Excellent or Very Good, Statistically speaking
+2 to +3	Good fit, Statistically speaking
+3 to +4	Marginally Acceptable Fit, Statistically Speaking
+4 to +5	Doubtful Fit, Statistically Speaking

$(Z)^2$ or Chi Square Test

0 to <8	Better than Perfect Fit, Statistically Speaking
8	Perfect Fit, Statistically Speaking
>8 to <15	Excellent or Very Good Fit, Statistically Speaking
>15 to <25	Acceptable Fit, Statistically Speaking
>25 to <35	Very Questionable Fit, Statistically Speaking

Remember the phrase, "Better than Perfect Fit, Statistically speaking".

Now, as we examine the graph (below) for ***Abundance of Elements in the Earth's Sea,*** we can see that the Z scores in the second column from the right are all below one (1) except for one (z) score of 1.06 for First Digit 9. Therefore, for the basic Standard Deviation (Z) scores, we see that they fall in the "Better than Perfect Fit" category. This is even more amazing when you consider that, as stated before, this is statistically impossible given the extremely small population of only 81.

Let us now see what the Chi Square (Z^2) score is and compare it to the Interpretation chart above.

First Digit	Fourth Order- Theoretical Proportion	$\overline{X}$ Theoretical Population	X Actual Population	X- $\overline{X}$	ESD	(Z) $\dfrac{X-\overline{X}}{ESD}$	(Z)^2
1	.3010	24	23	-1	4.13	-0.24	0.06
2	.1761	14	16	+2	3.43	**+0.58**	0.34
3	.1249	10	10	0	2.97	0.00	0.00
4	.0969	8	9	+1	2.66	+0.38	0.14
5	.0792	6	6	0	2.43	0.00	0.00
6	.0670	5	6	+1	2.25	+0.44	0.19
7	.0580	5	5	0	2.10	0.00	0.00
8	.0512	4	4	0	1.98	0.00	0.00
9	.0458	4	2	-2	1.88	**-1.06**	1.12
Totals	1.0000	(80)	81			$\Sigma(Z)^{2=}$	**1.85**
						chi-square	**1.66**

Abundance of Elements in the Earth's Sea

ESD

First Digit

1- $\sqrt{.2104 \times 81}$ = $\sqrt{17.04}$ = 4.13

2- $\sqrt{.1451 \times 81}$ = $\sqrt{11.75}$ = 3.43

3- $\sqrt{.1093 \times 81}$ = $\sqrt{8.85}$ = 2.97

4- $\sqrt{.0875 \times 81}$ = $\sqrt{7.09}$ = 2.66

5- $\sqrt{.0729 \times 81}$ = $\sqrt{5.90}$ = 2.43

6- $\sqrt{.0625 \times 81}$ = $\sqrt{5.06}$ = 2.25

7- $\sqrt{.0546 \times 81}$ = $\sqrt{4.42}$ = 2.10

8- $\sqrt{.0486 \times 81}$ = $\sqrt{3.94}$ = 1.98

9- $\sqrt{.0437 \times 81}$ = $\sqrt{3.54}$ = 1.88

Unbelievably it is only 1.66 (at the bottom of the last column on the right) remembering that anything less than 8 is again "Better than Perfect Fit".

> *"Once is an instance. Twice may be an accident. But three or more times makes a pattern."* — *Diane Ackerman*

Here is where it gets very interesting. The probability of the measurements of one (1) aspect of nature following a predetermined designated precise universal law of nature makes the happening of chance <u>nearly zero</u>!

Abundance of Elements in the Earth's Sea Chart[41]
Collected near the surface (in mg/L); Values represent the median of reported measurements. (Excluding DissolvedGases)

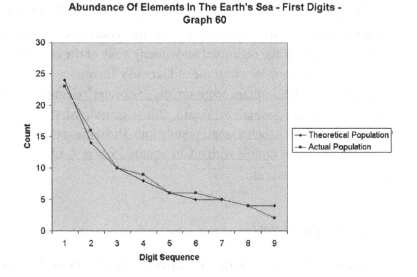

Abundance Of Elements In The Earth's Sea - First Digits - Graph 60

Again, the probability of the measurements of one (1) aspect of nature following a predetermined, designated, precise universal law of nature makes the happening of chance <u>nearly zero</u>! What evolutionists will say is that even with the Lottery, with odds up to 150 million or more, someone eventually wins. Therefore, under this probability, it could happen (at least once). The probability of this situation happening by chance a <u>second time is zero,</u> practically speaking.[42] So, using the Lottery example above, the odds here (of two random aspects of nature following a natural law) would be 150 million x 150 million or 2.25 x 10^{12} or 1 in 225 quadrillion. Not such good odds. The probability of this same situation happening by chance a <u>third time is beyond zero,</u> practically speaking! This number is simply too large to comprehend.

Please keep these statements in mind as we progress through the next few examples.

Solid Matter

Why is the application of the Law of First Digits to the Elements of Solid Matter (Earth's Crust) and the Elements of Liquid Matter (Seawater) so significant and important concerning the Theory of Darwinian Evolution? Because we are demonstrating the universality of the Law of First Digits as it reveals the organized and orderly array of the elements in matter, which are the opposite of those of Darwin's Theory.

Please note the Chi Square score on the "Seawater" example above is 1.66, well below a "perfect" fit. Again, this is considered statistically impossible especially for such a small population. The same status applies to the "Earth's Crust" example with a Chi Square score of 4.49, still well below a statistical "perfect" fit.

Are you intrigued yet?

Abundance of Elements in the Earth's Crust.[43] *Found in the Continental Crust (in mg/kg) equivalent to parts per million by mass.*

First Digit	Fourth Order - Theoretical Proportion	Theoretical Population	X Actual Population	$X - \overline{X}$	ESD	$\dfrac{(Z)}{\dfrac{X - \overline{X}}{ESD}}$	$(Z)^2$
1	0.3010	26	25	-1	4.30	-0.23	0.05
2	0.1761	15	18	3	3.57	0.84	0.71
3	0.1249	11	10	-1	3.10	-0.32	0.10
4	0.0969	9	7	-2	2.77	-0.72	0.52
5	0.0792	7	9	2	2.53	0.79	0.62
6	0.0670	6	3	-3	2.35	-1.28	1.64
7	0.0580	5	4	-1	2.19	-0.46	0.21
8	0.0512	5	7	2	2.07	0.97	0.94
9	0.0458	4	5	1	1.96	0.51	0.26
Totals	1.0000	88	88			$\Sigma(Z)^2=$	5.05
						chi-square	4.49

$$\underline{ESD}$$

First Digit					
1 -	$\sqrt{.2104 \times 88}$	=	$\sqrt{18.52}$	=	4.30
2 -	$\sqrt{.1451 \times 88}$	=	$\sqrt{12.77}$	=	3.57
3 -	$\sqrt{.1093 \times 88}$	=	$\sqrt{9.62}$	=	3.10
4 -	$\sqrt{.0875 \times 88}$	=	$\sqrt{7.70}$	=	2.77
5 -	$\sqrt{.0729 \times 88}$	=	$\sqrt{6.42}$	=	2.53
6 -	$\sqrt{.0625 \times 88}$	=	$\sqrt{5.50}$	=	2.35
7 -	$\sqrt{.0546 \times 88}$	=	$\sqrt{4.80}$	=	2.19
8 -	$\sqrt{.0486 \times 88}$	=	$\sqrt{4.28}$	=	2.07
9 -	$\sqrt{.0437 \times 88}$	=	$\sqrt{3.85}$	=	1.96

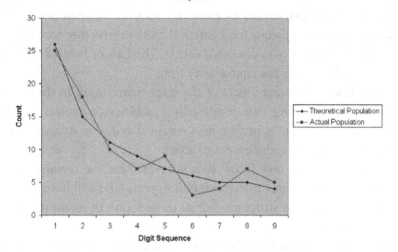

Abundance Of Elements In The Earth's Crust - First Digits - Graph 64

First, let us examine what we know in light of what evolutionists are telling us. The elements of atoms are the "building blocks" of all solid and liquid matter.

Secondly, Darwinian Evolution says, in its simplified form, that the combination of elements or atoms in the earth's crust and seawater through Natural Selection slowly evolved into more complex forms of chemical matter and life beings, including man.

Thirdly, for Darwin's Natural Selection theory to work there would have to be a dependence upon an initial chaotic array or disordered arrangement of the elements or atoms of matter, i.e., earth's crust and saltwater, according to the Theory of Darwinian Evolution.

However, as we just saw, the application of the Law of First Digits to the elements or atoms of the earth's crust and seawater prove scientifically that the initial elements or atoms were not and are not in a chaotic array or disordered arrangement. Instead, they were and are in an ordered or organized arrangement that follows a precise mathematical formula that is a true natural law of science.

Thus, we have exposed a fatal flaw in the theory of Darwinian Evolution in its application to the world as it is. It is only reasonable and logical to conclude that the theory of Darwinian Evolution could not be considered as an explanation for the origin of any species, most of all humanity.

The Law of First Digits not only proves that matter has order or structure but also proves that the same matter that existed in the alleged beginning of the Darwinian evolutionary natural selection process 4.0 billion years ago, had precise mathematical order or structure according to the Law of Invariability as discussed earlier. The Law of Invariability says the Laws of Nature do not change over time.

In addition, the exact aspect of the same matter used in the alleged evolutionary beginning that supposedly combines or evolves, i.e. the elements or atoms had a precise mathematical order or structure as to collective qualities of each element or atom.

Furthermore, we now know that samples from the remains of the combination of that same matter 4.0 billion years later still have a precise mathematical order or structure, just as those found in moon rocks and meteorites today.

Therefore, Darwin Evolution's natural selection in nature could <u>not</u> be a blind force of physics. A blind force would have <u>no</u> predictable or predetermined beginning, process, direct or end result concerning any aspect of matter.

The Law of First Digits requires a precise, mathematical, predictable or predetermined beginning, process, direction and end result concerning an important aspect of matter involving the collective quantities of elements or atoms for certain designated matter. The matter used by Darwinian Evolutionists in their flawed theory included newly formed rocks in the earth's crust and water in the earth's seas. This matter was not in disorder or in a chaotic structure at the elemental or atomic level as to collective quantities at the beginning, during the process of direction or at the end result.

Here is a revealing quote from a world renowned mathematical genius relating Chi Square scores to population size:

> "A Chi Square score that is too small would mean that the data was more uniform than what is expected by chance indicating a second order fake or manipulation."

Statistics and Truth, Ramanujan [44] *Memorial Lectures, International CoOperative*

Publishing House

In plain English, a too small Chi Square calculation result shows that something outside of chance has caused an influence in the applications shown here.

Another way of saying it is that the data used for each of the elements must have somehow been manipulated or changed in order to appear more uniform than natural in the applications to the earth's crust, seawater and gaseous vapor (below). Obviously, humankind could not have accomplished this manipulation of these varied elements of matter; therefore, some outside force must have caused this unique situation to occur. You are free to arrive at your own conclusion concerning what constitutes this outside force.

I trust your interest is now peaked.

Gaseous Matter (Vapor)

Let us now look at the constants for gases found in our atmosphere and see how they conform to Benford.

From the charts below you can see an incredibly close fit of 0.95, which again is better than perfect fit on the Chi Square Score chart.

Vander Waals Constants for Gasses[45]

First Digit	Fourth Order - Theoretical Proportion	$\overline{X}$ Theoretical Population	X Actual Population	$X - \overline{X}$	ESD	$\dfrac{(Z)}{\dfrac{X - \overline{X}}{ESD}}$	$(Z)^2$
1	0.3010	26	28	2	4.25	0.47	0.22
2	0.1761	15	14	-1	3.53	-0.28	0.08
3	0.1249	11	10	-1	3.07	-0.33	0.11
4	0.0969	8	9	1	2.74	0.36	0.13
5	0.0792	7	8	1	2.50	0.40	0.16
6	0.0670	6	5	-1	2.32	-0.43	0.18
7	0.0580	5	4	-1	2.17	-0.46	0.21
8	0.0512	4	4	0	2.04	0.00	0.00
9	0.0458	4	4	0	1.94	0.00	0.00
Totals	1.0000	86	86			$\sum(Z)^2 =$	1.09
						chi-square	0.95

ESD

First Digit

1 -	$\sqrt{.2104 \times 86}$	=	$\sqrt{18.09}$	=	4.25
2 -	$\sqrt{.1451 \times 86}$	=	$\sqrt{12.48}$	=	3.53
3 -	$\sqrt{.1093 \times 86}$	=	$\sqrt{9.40}$	=	3.07
4 -	$\sqrt{.0875 \times 86}$	=	$\sqrt{7.53}$	=	2.74
5 -	$\sqrt{.0729 \times 86}$	=	$\sqrt{6.27}$	=	2.50
6 -	$\sqrt{.0625 \times 86}$	=	$\sqrt{5.38}$	=	2.32
7 -	$\sqrt{.0546 \times 86}$	=	$\sqrt{4.70}$	=	2.17
8 -	$\sqrt{.0486 \times 86}$	=	$\sqrt{4.18}$	=	2.04
9 -	$\sqrt{.0437 \times 86}$	=	$\sqrt{3.76}$	=	1.94

(bar a L2/mol2)

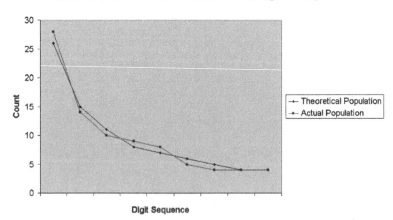

Vander Waals Constants For Gases - First Digits - Graph 69

Fundamental Physical Constants

How do the Fundamental Physical Constants[46] work with the Law of First Digits? Physical Constants are the set or constant values of different observed aspects of nature that are invariant, i.e. they are the same today as they were when matter and their attendant physical laws were first created.

Some more notable examples out of a total of 191 (this number is still debatable depending on whether some are considered dimensionless or not) include:

1. The speed of light in a vacuum c, c_o
2. The Newtonian Constant of Gravitation G
3. Magnetic Constant μ_o
4. Faraday Constant F
5. Neutron Mass m_n

When we chart these Fundamental Physical Constants, we find the same type of pattern as with the three tests above. Not surprisingly, they also fit the logarithmic distribution of the Law of First Digits. An interesting note: since it is supposedly statistically impossible to verify Benford's law using small data sets according to Hill, Nigrini and others, our set of 191 population (not sample) is impressive; but just as impressive is a study done by John Burke and Eric Kincanon utilizing only a sample set of 20 physical constants (choosing only the more well-known ones as mentioned above by their symbol to see if they would match the law. What was remarkable about the results was that there was any apparent agreement at all. Looking at the percentage occurrence of units, the most frequently occurring first digit is 1, although the overall agreement was far from exact. It was, however, surprising that the values are not randomly distributed and that they show some tendency to follow an empirical relation found independently of the set.[47]

Fundamental Physical Constants
CRC Handbook of Chemistry and Physics→ pp. 12 thru 19
83rd Edition 20022003

First Digit	Fourth Order— Theoretical Proportion	$\overline{X}$ Theoretical Population	X Actual Population	X - $\overline{X}$	ESD	(Z) $\dfrac{X-X}{ESD}$	(Z)^2
1	.3010	57	66	+9	6.34	**+1.42**	2.02
2	.1761	34	38	+4	5.26	+0.76	0.58
3	.1249	24	19	-5	4.57	—1.09	1.19
4	.0969	19	16	-3	4.09	—0.73	0.53
5	.0792	15	15	0	3.89	0.00	0.00
6	.0670	13	13	0	3.46	0.00	0.00
7	.0580	11	7	-4	3.23	— **1.24**	1.54
8	.0512	10	8	-2	3.05	-0.66	0.44
9	.0458	9	9	0	2.89	0.00	0.00
Totals	1.0000	(192)	191			$\sum(Z)^2$=	6.30
						chi square	5.25

ESD

First Digit

1— $\sqrt{.2104 \times 191}$ = $\sqrt{40.19}$ = 6.34

2— $\sqrt{.1451 \times 191}$ = $\sqrt{27.71}$ = 5.26

3— $\sqrt{.1093 \times 191}$ = $\sqrt{20.88}$ = 4.57

4— $\sqrt{.0875 \times 191}$ = $\sqrt{16.71}$ = 4.09

5— $\sqrt{.0729 \times 191}$ = $\sqrt{15.13}$ = 3.89

6— $\sqrt{.0625 \times 191}$ = $\sqrt{11.94}$ = 3.46

7— $\sqrt{.0546 \times 191}$ = $\sqrt{10.43}$ = 3.23

8— $\sqrt{.0486 \times 191}$ = $\sqrt{9.28}$ = 3.05

9— $\sqrt{.0437 \times 191}$ = $\sqrt{8.35}$ = 2.89

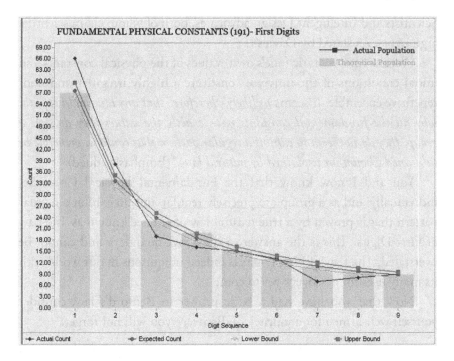

As you can also see in this result, the Chi Square score (Z^2) for the Fundamental Physical Constants of 5.25 is still better than a perfect fit of 8. It is interesting to note that Darwinian Evolutionists and the world scientific community generally agree that at least 30 of these known constants have to be precisely on the money for life to exist and 60 for the universe to function as it does. For some, however, this is proof enough for the argument of a "Supreme Being" or "Intelligent Designer", but to the Evolutionists, this proof is just a freak of nature; they do say, however, that if you can find any related order among all 191 fundamental physical constants, then they would have to reconsider their position. *Is that the same as "eating crow"?*

Now, we know that in addition to the required, precise, exact values of the Physical Constants, those values collectively must follow the precise order of The Law of First Digits.

Collectively, these scientific facts thus far prove that *The Organized Universe* is the correct "theory". Now, it should be clear that our research and findings constitute a quantum leap beyond that of the Creation

Scientists and Intelligent Design advocates, both of whom claim scientific arguments. As stated by Davies[48]:

"Yet the idiosyncratic (one's own) values of the physical constants and initial conditions of the universe constitute a highly irregular and non-repetitive ensemble. It seems *unlikely, therefore" that any law could explain why all the fundamental constants have exactly the values they do....As a group, they do not seem to exhibit a regular pattern that could in principle be subsumed (shown) or explained by natural law."* (Emphasis added)

You and I now know that the Fundamental Physical Constants individually and as a group are precisely regular and do exhibit a regular pattern that is proven by a true natural law of science known as The Law of First Digits. This is the answer to the above quandary and cannot be overstated. The Law of First Digits is indeed ubiquitous in our world with its many uses for discovery yet to come.

Now that you have had a basic primer in Benford's law, consider yourself well-armed for a journey of discovery you will not forget.

CHAPTER 4

Applying the Law of First Digits as a Measuring Stick to the Holy Scriptures of the Bible

"The heavens declare the glory of God; and the firmament showeth his handiwork. Their line (Heb. *Kav*—a measuring line or rule) *is gone out through all the earth."*
Psalm 19:1, 4a

"For the invisible things of him (God) from the creation of the world are clearly seen, being understood by the things (Universe and planet Earth) that are made...."
Romans 1:20

Other than the everyday witness of the miracle of nature where the evidence of intelligent design is everywhere and yet appears obvious to the eye, but with complexity that overwhelms the imagination, one is tempted to ask how would God reveal Himself to humankind in the form of a more direct proof—particularly an indisputable proof such as one that is mathematical?

We mentioned in Chapter 1 many of the forms of the most commonly known "biblical proofs" from prophesy, archeology, historical documents, geology, and archeology. However, none of the examples from these categories pertain to the Bible as a whole, but rather are validations of a particular verse or statement that subsequently was proven true, or physical artifacts subsequently found and verified.

According to the Scripture above, "the invisible things ...are clearly seen" meaning that the proof or revelation of God's creation may be hidden, but hidden in plain sight. This would appear to exclude intricate formulas requiring sophisticated computing programs to interpret any such hidden message as is claimed in the highly publicized Bible Codes, also discussed in Chapter 1. One would have to ask how such intricate and hidden knowledge would be accessible to the average person. On the other hand, is it possible that an easily *detectable pattern* found within "... all the invisible things of him (God) from the creation..." would be His way of revealing not only the symmetry of truth in all of nature but also in his written Word?

This is what we will explore in this chapter.

There are many religious books claiming to be God's truth. If God wanted us to know if a message were truly from Him, He would have given us a way to verify it. Certainly there are many forms of this revelation. The most common proof provided is that of prophesy and is the first one that comes to mind for most people. In the Christian Bible, the Scripture is clear as who God claims to be as well as His ability to see into the future. As stated in Isaiah 42:8-9:

> *"I am the LORD, that is my name! I will not give my name to another or my praise to idols.*
>
> *See, the former things have taken place, and new things I declare; before they spring into being I announce them to you"*

This passage bears examination. "… the former things are come to pass"; that is, the former things which he had foretold. This is the evidence to which he appeals in proof that he alone was God, and this is the basis on which he calls upon them to believe that what he had predicted in regard to future things would also come to pass. He had by his prophets foretold events which had now been fulfilled, and this should lead them to confide in him alone as the true God.

"And new things I declare"—things pertaining to future events, relating to the coming of the Messiah, and to the universal prevalence of his religion in the world.

"…before they spring into being…" There is here a beautiful image. The metaphor is taken from plants and flowers, the word צמח tsâmach properly referring to the springing up of plants, or to their sending out shoots, buds, or flowers. The phrase literally means, 'before they begin to germinate,' that is, before there are any indications of life, or growth in the plant. The sense is that God predicted the future events before there was anything by which it might be inferred that such occurrences would take place. It was not done by mere sagacity—as men like Burke and Canning may sometimes predict future events with great probability by marking certain political indications or developments. God did this when there were no such indications, and when it must have been done by mere omniscience. In this respect, all his predictions differ from the conjectures of man, and from all the reasoning, which are founded on mere sagacity. [49]

Prophecy through God's prescience is further illustrated by these related passages:

Isaiah 43:19
"Behold, I will do something new, Now it will spring forth;
Will you not be aware of it? I will even make a roadway in
the wilderness, Rivers in the desert."

Isaiah 48:3
"I declared the former things long ago And they went forth
from My mouth, and I proclaimed them. Suddenly I acted,
and they came to pass."

Isaiah 48:6
"You have heard; look at all this. And you, will you not
declare it? I proclaim to you new things from this time,
Even hidden things which you have not known."

Naturalism and the Theory of Evolution

Modern day scientific naturalists hold the view that nature is fundamental and self-sufficient, having long since overturned the ancient understanding and logic that God was recognizable in creation. Thus was born Darwin's Theory of Evolution in the mid-19th century profoundly influencing conventional scientific thought by giving us a creation story where God was absent and a theory that all life developed from naturalistic determination (i.e. undirected natural processes by chance) based on his collateral theory of natural selection.

Prior to our first book, *The Organized Universe,* the best and most ardent challenge of this long held naturalism had been the theory of Intelligent Design (ID). There, William Dembski states that many Christians accept that God's design is accessible only through the eyes of faith, but argues on behalf of ID that God's design is also accessible to scientific inquiry. He then lays out the case that design is empirically detectable and can be so detected through observation, provided, however, that two features are present[50]:

- Complexity – which guarantees that the object in question is not so simple that it can readily be attributed to chance, and
- Specification – guaranteeing that the object exhibits the *right sort of pattern associated with intelligent causes.*

  A short analogy will make this clear. A single letter of the alphabet is specified without being complex. A long sequence of random letters is complex without being specified. A Shakespearean sonnet is both complex and specified. Therefore, specified complexity is how we detect design empirically.

This is the view of a new generation of theistic scholars who believe that this 'naturalistic' creation story will be replaced by the theory of Intelligent Design as it purports to tear down the edifices of evolutionary thought built on a foundation of undirected natural causes.

But wait! That effort has already failed. As discussed in detail in *The Organized Universe,* ID proponents have failed in toto to convince the courts that their theory is science based as opposed to a thinly disguised version of 'creation lite'.

On the other hand, we have accomplished this goal of upending the theory of evolution and its naturalistic determinism. And it was done with *The Organized Universe*. <u>We also believe that God's design is accessible to scientific inquiry</u>. By using Benford's Law of First Digits as our scientific tool, we tore down the edifice of natural selection in evolution and the rest of the foundation of evolution crumbles as a result.

As stated at the beginning, the thesis of this book is to use the same scientific methodology to prove the authentication of the Holy Bible as the written Word of God, just as it claims to be. Of all the so-called Holy Writings, only the Bible authenticates itself like this. In fact God challenges anyone else claiming to be like Him to prove himself this way. The Bible is the only religious scripture of any religion which claims to be the Holy written Word of the one and only God of the universe.

When we review the charts and graphs presented in Chapter 3 pertaining to both natural elements and unrelated natural lists of life events on earth, we see a near perfect fit of the data to the established geometric and logarithmic curve of Benford's Law of First Digits, thereby noting their conformity to the accuracy of the law. This proof lays the groundwork for expanding our reach (and curiosity) to include related phenomenon in the written word. Will this universal law of science, this "law of laws" as created by God from the moment of creation, reveal this same Divine pattern in the only object purportedly handed down over the centuries through various scribes and prophets— i.e., the Holy Bible?

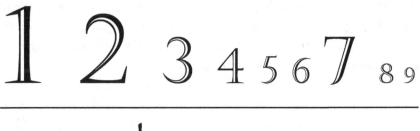

Holy Scripture

However, before we begin, let me share with you what we found at the onset as we began to analyze the Holy Scriptures of the Bible for its conformity to Benford's Law. What we found was both fascinating and, in a surprising twist, a conformation of why the Bible is truly the inspired Word of God.

The Holiness and Majesty of the Number Seven (7)

While charting and graphing the first significant digits found in the text of both the Old Testament and the New Testament, just as we had done with various elements in nature and unrelated natural lists of life events on earth, a peculiar thing happened when we got to the number "seven" (7). When calculating its frequency as a significant "first digit" (first order theoretical proportion), instead of the total number of sevens (population) corresponding to an approximate 2.3% frequency, as dictated by the Law of First Digits, the frequency percentage turned out to be 16.1% *or exactly seven (7) times that of the theoretical.* This spike at the 7 position is easily seen in the graph below comparing the theoretical frequencies to the actual frequencies or proportions for the Bible as a whole. Remember, the spike you see for the number seven is *exactly* 7 times that of the non-adjusted theoretical line.

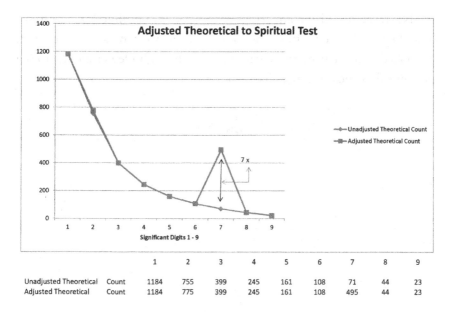

		1	2	3	4	5	6	7	8	9
Unadjusted Theoretical	Count	1184	755	399	245	161	108	71	44	23
Adjusted Theoretical	Count	1184	775	399	245	161	108	495	44	23

At first glance we were very concerned that either our calculations were wrong or that the Bible text was somehow flawed and simply did not conform to Benford's Law after all, thus casting doubt on our theory. As you can imagine, this was very disappointing and troublesome.

We first looked at just the Old Testament to see how it conformed to the Benford theoretical curve based on the number of First Significant Digits found.

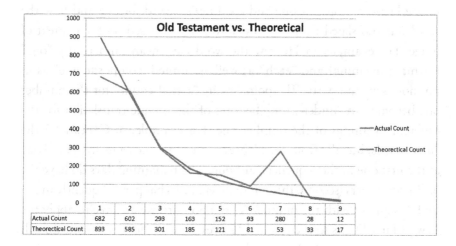

	1	2	3	4	5	6	7	8	9
Actual Count	682	602	293	163	152	93	280	28	12
Theorectical Count	893	585	301	185	121	81	53	33	17

Next, we looked at comparing various books of both testaments to see how they conformed within each testament as well to each other. First, we looked at comparing the Torah (Genesis through Deuteronomy) to the theoretical as shown in the chart below:

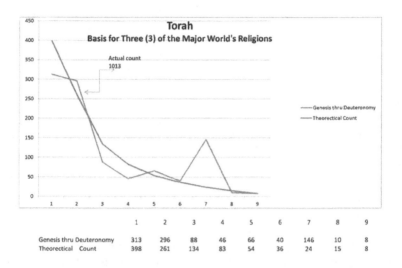

	1	2	3	4	5	6	7	8	9
Genesis thru Deuteronomy	313	296	88	46	66	40	146	10	8
Theorectical Count	398	261	134	83	54	36	24	15	8

Here there are two things that are noteworthy. The first is the obvious "spike" for the number seven (7) which we have encountered at every turn. More on this later. Secondly, there is a noticeable divergence in the actual count for the number "one'" as compared to the theoretical count for number one. This occurs because of the unique differences in the Hebrew word for one and the English word for one and how the word was translated from Hebrew into English based on the context of usage. For example, in Hebrew the word can mean numerically "one" (its main meaning) and "each" as well as "united, composite one" as in no more separate parts. The point is our "actual count" for the number one becomes an "undercount" because of the unique translation for the different meanings of the number one. For example, in Genesis 1:5 the "first" day is, literally from the Hebrew, "day one" (i.e., a really special day as the first one in the sequence), although the remaining days do have the ordinal numbers (second, third, fourth, etc.; this happens frequently in the Old Testament with the number "one".) So until we are able to apply the Law of First Digits to the original Hebrew of the Old Testament, we will have to recognize and adjust for these anomalies.

Next, we performed the same analysis for the New Testament as to the total number of First Significant Digits we found and compared them to the theoretical of Benford. The following graph tells the story:

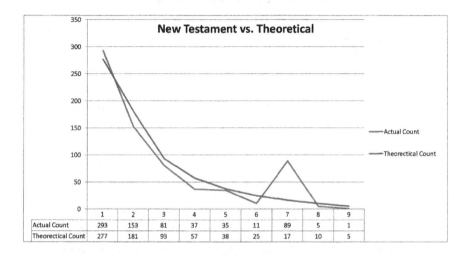

	1	2	3	4	5	6	7	8	9
Actual Count	293	153	81	37	35	11	89	5	1
Theorectical Count	277	181	93	57	38	25	17	10	5

Again, we see almost perfect conformity to the law with the exception of the standout number seven (7), which will be discussed in detail below, but without a discrepancy for the number one. This we assume is because the Greek translations were closer to the English meanings than were those of the Hebrew.

When we superimpose the above two graphs (see below) of both testaments, we again see the identical spike in both for the number seven (7).

OT Count	682	602	293	163	152	93	280	28	12	2305
NT Count	293	153	81	37	35	11	89	5	1	705

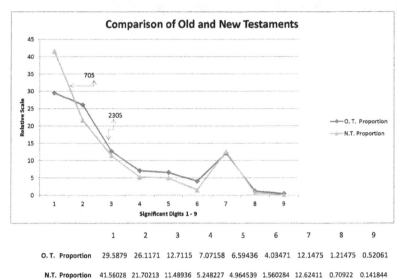

	1	2	3	4	5	6	7	8	9
O. T. Proportion	29.5879	26.1171	12.7115	7.07158	6.59436	4.03471	12.1475	1.21475	0.52061
N.T. Proportion	41.56028	21.70213	11.48936	5.248227	4.964539	1.560284	12.62411	0.70922	0.141844

Still perplexed and concerned, we decided to further test various combinations of books in the Bible and see this conformity to a "spiked" seven was consistent.

A curious thing happened on the way to the truth. When we broke down our analysis of the Biblical text (again using the KJV) from analyzing the entire text to looking at just single books and/or by combinations of different books, this seemingly anomalous spike for the number seven (7) remained amazingly consistent for every separate analysis we performed. We were shocked but hopeful there were valid reasons for these results.

For example, consider an analysis of Matthew through Acts plus Revelation as shown in the following graph:

Matthew thru Acts plus Revelation

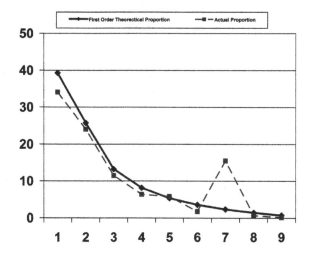

We were now becoming hopeful as again we saw the same odd spike for number seven but with the remaining comparisons being nearly perfect,

Notice in the graph below that when we adjust the number seven values to the natural state (i.e., we divide the supernatural population of 88 by 7 = 12.57 or 13 rd. as shown in the statistical chart analysis following the graph), the distribution conforms to a score of 10.4, which is an excellent or very good fit, statistically speaking (see page 67 for definitions):

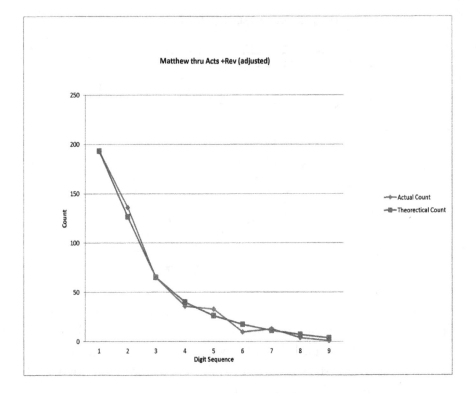

IMPORTED TEST DATA

Matthew thru Acts + Revelation

Digit	Count	% of Total
1	193	39.31%
2	136	27.70%
3	65	13.24%
4	36	7.33%
5	33	6.72%
6	10	2.04%
7	13	2.65%
8	4	0.81%
9	1	0.20%
	491	

First Digit	First Order Theoretical Proportion	$\ddot{X}$ Theoretical Population	X Actual Population	$X-\ddot{X}$ 2 decimals	$X-\ddot{X}$ Rounded	ESD	(Z) $\frac{X-\ddot{X}}{ESD}$	$(Z)^2$
1	0.3932	193	193	-0.06	0.00	10.16	0.00	0.00
2	0.2576	126	136	9.52	10.00	8.44	1.18	1.40
3	0.1327	65	65	-0.16	0.00	7.33	0.00	0.00
4	0.0815	40	36	-4.02	-4.00	6.55	-0.61	0.37
5	0.0534	26	33	6.78	7.00	5.98	1.17	1.37
6	0.0358	18	10	-7.58	-8.00	5.54	-1.44	2.09
7*	0.0235	12	13	1.46	1.00	5.18	0.19	0.04
8	0.0146	7	4	-3.17	-3.00	4.88	-0.61	0.38
9	0.0077	4	1	-2.78	-3.00	4.63	-0.65	0.42
Totals	1.0000	491	491				$\sum(Z)^2=$	6.06
							Chi-Square	10.42291851

Note: Digit 7 had a population of 88 which was divided by 7 = 12.57 or 13 rd. This adjusts the population to 491 for the "natural state".

ESD
Estimated Standard Deviation

First Digit	CONSTANT	ACTUAL POPULATION	SUM	SQ RT
1	0.2104	491	103.31	10.16
2	0.1451	491	71.24	8.44
3	0.1093	491	53.67	7.33
4	0.0875	491	42.96	6.55
5	0.0729	491	35.79	5.98
6	0.0625	491	30.69	5.54
7	0.0546	491	26.81	5.18
8	0.0486	491	23.86	4.88
9	0.0437	491	21.46	4.63

Another revealing and amazing comparison was the overlaying of graphs between Matthew through John plus revelation (NT) with Genesis through Deuteronomy (OT):

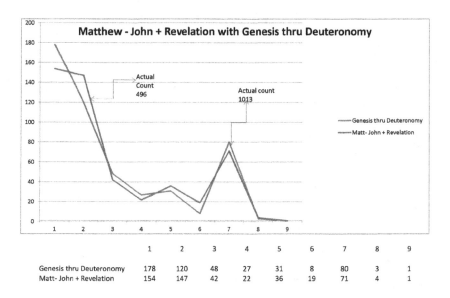

	1	2	3	4	5	6	7	8	9
Genesis thru Deuteronomy	178	120	48	27	31	8	80	3	1
Matt- John + Revelation	154	147	42	22	36	19	71	4	1

Amazingly, we have the same conformity as before: *an identical spike for number seven as well as for the rest of the numbers.* Remember, these books were written hundreds of centuries apart.

Again, if we adjust the number seven to the "natural state" as described above, we see an almost identical conformity.

So the question then became, "What is so special about the number "seven (7)" in the Bible and why is this anomaly the same in every analysis? What is its relevance to our analysis and to the divinity of the Bible itself? The answers were rather surprising.

After digging deeper, we found that there is something very special indeed about the number seven (7) and its special prominence within the Bible. But it also became evident during our research that many of the numbers in the Bible have deeper prophetic or spiritual significance. Both in the Old and New Testaments, numbers reveal hidden concepts and meanings that commonly escape the casual reader. And throughout history, men with great minds, like Augustine, Isaac Newton, and Leonardo Da Vinci, showed more than just a passing curiosity regarding the importance of biblical numbers. Once more, Jesus said, *"But the very hairs of your head are all numbered"* (Matthew 10:30). Obviously, Biblical numbers should be seriously considered.

Although there are 12 numbers in the Bible that stand out in this regard (1, 2, 3, 4, 5, 6, 7, 10, 12, 40, 50, and 70), there is no doubt that the number seven (7) is the "prince" of numbers when it comes to its unmatched significance and prominence in the Bible.

We discovered that the main reason for this significance is that the number seven (7) is the symbolic representation or sign of the Word of God; it also represents *perfection, divine authorship,* divine worship, *completion,* obedience, and rest. This "prince" of Biblical numbers is used 562 times throughout the Bible, including its derivatives (e.g., seventh, sevens, etc.). (See Genesis 2:1-4, Psalm 119:164, and Exodus 20:8-11 for just a few of the examples.)

Surprisingly, the number seven (7) is also the most common number in biblical prophecy, occurring 42 times in Daniel and Revelation alone. For example, in Revelation there are seven churches, seven spirits, seven golden candlesticks, seven stars, seven lamps, seven seals, seven horns, seven eyes, seven angels, seven trumpets, seven thunders, seven thousand slain in a great earthquake, seven heads, seen crowns, seven last plagues, seen golden vials, seven mountains and seven kings.[51] You get the point.

You can now see what a powerful role the number seven (7) plays and how it gives a whole new meaning to the phrase, "lucky 7", even in today's world. As stated above, we found that within the context of its representation of the Word of God, the number seven (7) indicates a *completeness, wholeness, or perfection.* Therefore, if there is one number that exemplifies the essence of God himself, it would be this sublime number.

So, despite this sacred symbolism, does the number seven (7) spike anomaly represent a flaw in our proof?

We will go through this symbolism later in the chapter as well as proving that the supposedly anomalous spike in the number seven (7) on the charts above can be explained by the Holy Scriptures themselves. If we cannot explain away or justify this anomaly, then our theory of proving the authenticity of the Bible through Benford is flawed from the outset. So, let us dig a little deeper and see what this number seven (7) holds for us.

As is commonly known, the Bible is replete with references, symbols, direct statements and hidden uses and meanings regarding the number seven (7). Even when you look at just the compilation, construction, and organization of the Bible, you see the relationship to the number seven (7). For example, although English speakers often think of the Bible as containing 66 books—39 in the Old Testament and 27 in the New Testament books—the ancient Hebrew reckoning divided the Old Testament into only 22 books. Therefore, we can see that the Bible consist of a canon of 49 books—seven times seven—a number used throughout Scripture to indicate completion and perfection. In turn, the 49 books can be classified into seven subdivisions as shown in the Symmetry of the Scriptures. (Please see chart in the Appendixes)

The Number Seven (7) and the First Verse of the Bible

God started out with the very first verse of the Bible to make a statement to demonstrate His Divine Authorship, His Supernatural Authority. Through the author, Moses, God talks about space (heaven), time (a beginning) and matter (earth). "In the beginning, God created the Heaven and the Earth." Genesis 1:1. Bear in mind that this concept of space-time-matter or the space/time continuum was not discovered by science until the 20th century. Remember, Genesis was written over 30 centuries ago.

In our natural world today, we see the reflection of the number seven (7) in practically every aspect of our natural world. There are 7 continents, 7 oceans, 7 colors of a rainbow, 7 notes in a musical scale, 7 stars in the Big Dipper, 7 digits in our phone numbers since 7 digits in a row is the most that people can remember, 7 levels in the Periodic Table, etc.

But most striking is the incredible illustration of the number seven (7) describing 7 distinctive features of the number 7 just within the first sentence of the Bible. In the English translation, there are 10 words. In the original Hebrew, there are exactly 7 words. A short list makes the point:

- ❖ The total number of words = 7
- ❖ The total number of letters = 28 or 4 x 7

❖ The 3 leading main words or nouns (God, Heaven, Earth) consist of 14 letters or 2 x 7

❖ The shortest word is the middle word which has 7 letters

And it goes on with more examples.

Nowhere else in the Bible can this extraordinary reference to the number 7 be found? It is certainly hidden beneath the text for the casual reader of Hebrew, but is nonetheless available to all who do the research. This in itself indicates the Divine Touch of God.

Structure of the Bible around the number 7

Even more amazing is the fact that the entire Bible is to some degree organized around the number seven (7)—not just the repetition of the number, such as in bowls or lamps, of which there are over 600 examples—but rather as Dr. Ivan Panin found in 1890, that the heptadic structure, or the structure build around the number seven (7), *permeates the totality of Scripture because the number speaks of God's Divine perfection and perfect order.* Over the course of 50 years Panin generated 43,000 pages of handwritten discoveries involving the number seven (7) revealing the most amazing mathematical pattern hidden beneath the text of the Bible. One amazing fact is that Panin discovered 30 separate codes involving the number 7 in just the first verse of the Bible (Genesis 1: 1) as briefly touched on above.

But the most interesting of Panin's discoveries—and one that stands out—is the fact that the Greek vocabulary used in Matthew, and which is unique to Matthew, is an exact multiple of 7 and is found in no other Gospel; for example, you have a total of 42 unique words from the Greek, a multiple of 7 (42=7 x 6); also the total number of letters in those words is 126 or 7x18— another multiple of exactly7. Fascinated yet? So how is it possible that Mathew could have organized his writings in this unique way? He could not have orchestrated an agreement among the other Gospel writers to not use these particular Greek words or have all of their writings in front of him; or, maybe he simply wrote his gospel last. The problem with this theory is that this phenomenon is not only true for the Gospel of Matthew but it is also true for the Gospel of Mark…and Luke, and

John, and James, and Peter, and Jude and Paul. Each of these writers have vocabularies that are unique to them and that contain words that are an exact multiples of 7. This boggles the mind. How could this occur? Obviously, they all could not have written their Gospel last, so what does this mean? They must have been inspired and guided by something outside of themselves, something supernatural.

Other notable examples of the Number seven (7) found in the Bible are:

- God rested on the 7th day after 6 days of Creation. (Gen 2:2, 3; Ex 20:8-11)
- Enoch was the 7th from Adam (Jude 14)
- Clean beasts went into the ark by sevens. (Gen 7:2)
- The door of Noah's ark closed 7 days before the Flood. (Gen 7:9,10)
- Jacob worked 7 years, twice, for Rachel. (Gen 29:18-28)
- Pharaoh dreamed of 7 lean and 7 fat cows. (Gen 41:17-21)
- Waters of Egypt were blood for 7 days. (Gen 7:20,25)
- 7 was the number of times Jericho was marched around on the day the walls fell. (Joshua 6:4)
- 7 was the number of locks of hair Delilah shaved from Samson's head. (Judges 19:19)
- Years it took for Solomon to build the Temple was 7. (1 Kings 6:38)
- Shunammite's son when raised back to life sneezed 7 times. (2 Kings 4:35)
- Naaman washed 7 times in Jordan. (2 Kings 5:9-14)
- Nebuchadnezzar dwelt among the beasts for 7 years. (Dan 4:13-17, 28-34)
- 7 was the number of baskets of fragments left after feeding 4,000 (Matthew 15:37)
- Seven loaves and a few fishes to feed the 4000 men, besides the women and children. (Matt 15:34-36)
- 7 was the number of devils Jesus cast out of Mary Magdalene. (Mark 19:9)
- Seven stars. (Rev 1:16)
- Seven churches. (Rev 1:4. 11,20)
- Seven seals. (Rev 8:1)

- Seven trumpets. (Rev 8:2-8)
- Seven thunders. (Rev 10:3. 4)
- The 7 angels bringing the 7 last plagues. (Rev 15,16)
- Seven deacons in early church. (Acts 6:3-5)

Not to belabor the point, but apparently the Bible has a lot to say about the number seven (7).

A last example of the wisdom of the number seven (7) is found in God's design in nature. Just look at how God's accuracy may be observed in the hatching of eggs:

For example:

—the eggs of the potato bug hatch in 7 days;
—those of the canary in 14 days;
—those of the barnyard hen in 21 days;
—The eggs of ducks and geese hatch in 28 days;
—those of the mallard in 35 days;
—The eggs of the parrot and the ostrich hatch in 42 days.

(Notice, they are all divisible by seven, the number of days in a week!)

So, the question remains, how do we reconcile the supernatural population of the number seven (the "spike") with the theoretical distribution curve of Benford's law?

It bears repeating again that the number seven (7) represents "perfection" and that it is, among other things, one of the symbolic designations for the Word of God. Therefore, we contend that the Holy Scripture can explain the positive spike of number seven (7) with the following analysis:

1. Number seven (7) is one of the symbolic designations for the Word of God as illustrated below.
    a. Jesus Christ is referred to as the **Lamb of God**
       John 1:29 "...John the Baptist seeth Jesus...and saith, Behold the Lamb of God
       I Peter 1:19 "...the precious blood of Christ as of a lamb..."
    b. Jesus Christ is the **Word of God**

John 1:1, 14 "...the Word was God...And the Word was made flesh..."

Rev 19:13 "...His name is called the Word of God"

John 1:3 "All things were made by Him (Jesus Christ)..."

Heb 11:3 "...the worlds were framed by the Word of God..."

John 3:34 "...He whom God hath sent speaketh the Words of God" (the Word of God)

So, we learn that:

- Jesus Christ is Lamb
- Jesus Christ is Word of God
- Lamb is Word of God

Therefore, If a = b and
        If a = c
Then   b = c

c. The Lamb is the Word of God (see a and b above)
d. The Word of God has seven (7) horns (omnipotence), seven eyes (omniscience)...

and seven spirits of God (omnipresence).

(Rev 5:1 "a book...sealed with seven seals")

Rev 5:6 "...a Lamb (Word of God) as it had been slain, having seven horns and seven eyes, which are the seven spirits of God sent forth into all the earth."

Therefore, we confirm that the number seven (7) is one of the symbolic designations for the Word of God. God has stamped or sealed a divine seven-fold pattern on His revelation (Word of God) to confirm that it is His message to the believers of all generations!)

1. The Word of God is to be multiplied by seven (7).

   Psalms 12:6   "The Words of the Lord are pure words, like silver tried in the furnace of the earth, purified <u>seven times.</u>"NKJV

2. Seven (7) (Word of God) is to be multiplied by seven (7) and the product or answer is a purified or supernatural population.

3. Conversely, in order to obtain an unrefined natural population, the purified or supernatural population can be divided by seven (7).

Supernatural Population (Refined)	Divided by Seven (7) =	Natural Population (Unrefined)

You recall from Chapter __2_ that the Supernatural (or Theoretical) Population of Number seven (7) was approximately 2.3%; therefore if the actual frequency percentage of the number seven (7) is 16.1% (see graphs above), then the unrefined natural population would be $16.1/.023 = 7^{ii}$

The number seven (7) is also shown to be a *special signature of God* as revealed in the following passages:

"For behold the stone that I have laid before Joshua; upon one stone shall be seven eyes: behold, I will engrave the graving thereof, saith the Lord of hosts...

Zechariah 3: 9

The "stone" referred to here is symbolic of the Messiah.
The "seven (7)" eyes undoubtedly refer to the same thing
symbolized in Zech. 4: 10 and Rev. 5:6 below.

"...with those seven; they are the eyes of the Lord which
run to and fro through the whole earth."
Zechariah 4: 10

"...stood a Lamb as it had been slain, having seven horns and seven
eyes, which are the seven spirits of God sent forth into all the earth.
Revelation 5: 6

"...and there were seven lamps of fire burning before
the throne, which are the seven spirits of God."
Revelation 4: 5

"The words of the Lord are pure words, like silver tried
in the furnace of the earth, purified seven times.
Psalm 12:6

Applying the Law of First Digits to the Holy Scripture

Now that we have established that the number seven (7)—despite its apparent non-conformity to Benford's logarithmic curve—is in reality a "sign of God" representing perfection and completeness, and that the "Word of God is to be multiplied by 7," we can find other comparative proofs throughout the Bible.

Let us start with a simple comparison of the number of First Significant Digits found in the Old Testament to those found in the New Testament (KJV), we find a remarkable conformity as shown in the graph and chart below:

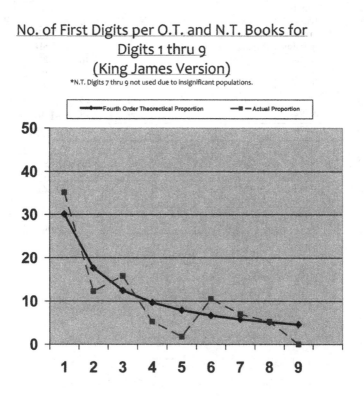

No. of First Digits per O.T. and N.T. Books for Digits 1 thru 9 (King James Version)
*N.T. Digits 7 thru 9 not used due to insignificant populations.

NO. OF FIRST DIGITS PER
O.T. AND N.T. * BOOKS FOR DIGITS 1 THRU 9
*N.T. DIGITS 7 THRU 9 NOT USED DUE TO INSIGNIFICANT POPULATIONS
(KING JAMES VERSION)

First Digit	Fourth Order-Theoretical Proportion	$\overline{X}$ Theoretical Population	X Actual Population	$X - \overline{X}$	ESD	(Z) $\dfrac{X-\overline{X}}{ESD}$	$(Z)^2$
1	.3010	17	20	+3	3.46	+0.87	0.76
2	.1761	10	7	-3	2.88	-1.04	1.08
3	.1249	7	9	+2	2.50	+0.80	0.64
4	.0969	6	3	-3	2.23	-1.35	1.82
5	.0792	5	1	-4	2.04	**-1.96**	3.84
6	.0670	4	6	+2	1.89	**+1.06**	1.12
7	.0580	3	4	+1	1.76	+0.57	0.32
8	.0512	3	3	0	1.66	0.00	0.00
9	.0458	3	4	+1	1.58	+0.64	0.41
Totals	1.0000	(58)	57			$\Sigma(Z)^2=$	**9.99**
						chi-square	**8.36**

ESD

First Digit

1- $\sqrt{.2104 \times 57}$ = $\sqrt{11.99}$ = 3.46

2- $\sqrt{.1451 \times 57}$ = $\sqrt{8.27}$ = 2.88

3- $\sqrt{.1093 \times 57}$ = $\sqrt{6.23}$ = 2.50

4- $\sqrt{.0875 \times 57}$ = $\sqrt{4.99}$ = 2.23

5- $\sqrt{.0729 \times 57}$ = $\sqrt{4.16}$ = 2.04

6- $\sqrt{.0625 \times 57}$ = $\sqrt{3.56}$ = 1.89

7- $\sqrt{.0546 \times 57}$ = $\sqrt{3.11}$ = 1.76

8- $\sqrt{.0486 \times 57}$ = $\sqrt{2.77}$ = 1.66

9- $\sqrt{.0437 \times 57}$ = $\sqrt{2.49}$ = 1.58

As you can see from the Chi Square score of 8.36, there is almost a perfect fit as any score below 8 is considered a better than perfect fit. How remarkable that God has infused all of His Holy Scripture with such a precise mathematical conformity to one of His own natural laws.

To broaden the test even further, we decided to pick some of the more well-known yet common words used in the New Testament, in both

English, Hebrew and Greek, to see how many times they were used in each book of the New Testament. We also measured them in *combination with each other* to see how the numbers conformed to the Law of First Digits. You will note in the following eleven (11) charts that all of them show a Chi Square score of <8, which as you recall is consider a better than perfect fit. Can this be just an amazing coincidence?

NO. OF TIMES THE WORD "FATHER(S)" (GOD) IN GREEK AND ENGLISH IS USED PER BOOK IN THE N.T. (KING JAMES VERSION FOR ENGLISH) STRONG'S CONCORDANCE

First Digit	Fourth Order-Theoretical Proportion	$\overline{X}$ Theoretical Population	X Actual Population	X - $\overline{X}$	ESD	(Z) $\dfrac{X-\overline{X}}{ESD}$	(Z)²
1	.3010	8	8	0	2.29	0.00	0.00
2	.1761	4	2	-2	1.91	**-1.05**	1.10
3	.1249	3	5	+2	1.65	+1.21	1.46
4	.0969	2	4	+2	1.48	+1.35	1.82
5	.0792	2	4	+2	1.35	**+1.48**	2.19
6	.0670	2	1	-1	1.25	-0.80	0.64
7	.0580	1	0	-1	1.17	-0.85	0.72
8	.0512	1	1	0	1.10	0.00	0.00
9	.0458	1	0	-1	1.04	-0.96	0.92
Totals	1.0000	(24)	25			Σ(Z)²=	**8.85**
						chi-square	**8.83**

ESD

First
Digit

1- √ .2104 x 25   =   √ 5.26   = 2.29

2- √ .1451 x 25   =   √ 3.63   = 1.91

3- √ .1093 x 25   =   √ 2.73   = 1.65

4- √ .0875 x 25   =   √ 2.19   = 1.48

5- √ .0729 x 25   =   √ 1.82   = 1.35

6- √ .0625 x 25   =   √ 1.56   = 1.25

7- √ .0546 x 25   =   √ 1.37   = 1.17

8- √ .0486 x 25   =   √ 1.22   = 1.10

9- √ .0437 x 25   =   √ 1.09   = 1.04

NO. OF TIMES THE WORD "JESUS" (CHRIST) IN ENGLISH IS USED PER BOOK OF N.T. (KING JAMES VERSION) STRONG'S CONCORDANCE

First Digit	Fourth Order-Theoretical Proportion	$\overline{X}$ Theoretical Population	X Actual Population	X - $\overline{X}$	ESD	(Z) $\dfrac{X-\overline{X}}{ESD}$	$(Z)^2$
1	.3010	8	11	+3	2.34	**+1.28**	1.64
2	.1761	5	7	+2	1.94	+1.03	1.06
3	.1249	3	1	-2	1.69	-1.18	1.39
4	.0969	3	1	-2	1.51	-1.32	1.74
5	.0792	2	1	-1	1.38	-0.72	0.52
6	.0670	2	1	-1	1.28	-0.78	0.61
7	.0580	2	2	0	1.19	0.00	0.00
8	.0512	1	0	-1	1.12	-0.89	0.79
9	.0458	1	2	+1	1.07	**+0.93**	0.86
Totals	1.0000	(27)	26			$\Sigma(Z)^2=$	**8.61**
						chi-square	**7.59**

ESD

First Digit

1- $\sqrt{.2104 \times 26}$ = $\sqrt{5.47}$ = 2.34

2- $\sqrt{.1451 \times 26}$ = $\sqrt{3.77}$ = 1.94

3- $\sqrt{.1093 \times 26}$ = $\sqrt{2.84}$ = 1.69

4- $\sqrt{.0875 \times 26}$ = $\sqrt{2.28}$ = 1.51

5- $\sqrt{.0729 \times 26}$ = $\sqrt{1.90}$ = 1.38

6- $\sqrt{.0625 \times 26}$ = $\sqrt{1.63}$ = 1.28

7- $\sqrt{.0546 \times 26}$ = $\sqrt{1.42}$ = 1.19

8- $\sqrt{.0486 \times 26}$ = $\sqrt{1.26}$ = 1.12

9- $\sqrt{.0437 \times 26}$ = $\sqrt{1.14}$ = 1.07

NO. OF TIMES THE WORD "JESUS" (CHRIST) IN GREEK IS USED PER BOOK OF N.T.

First Digit	Fourth Order-Theoretical Proportion	$\overline{X}$ Theoretical Population	X Actual Population	X - $\overline{X}$	ESD	(Z) $\dfrac{X-\overline{X}}{ESD}$	(Z)²
1	.3010	8	10	+2	2.34	+0.85	0.72
2	.1761	5	7	+2	1.94	+1.03	1.06
3	.1249	3	1	-2	1.69	**-1.18**	1.39
4	.0969	3	1	-2	1.51	-1.32	1.74
5	.0792	2	1	-1	1.38	-0.72	0.52
6	.0670	2	1	-1	1.28	-0.78	0.61
7	.0580	2	2	0	1.19	0.00	0.00
8	.0512	1	0	-1	1.12	-0.89	0.79
9	.0458	1	3	+2	1.07	**+1.87**	3.50
Totals	1.0000	(27)	26			$\sum(Z)^2=$ **10.33**	
						chi-square	**9.96**

ESD

First Digit

1- $\sqrt{.2104 \times 26}$ = $\sqrt{5.47}$ = 2.34

2- $\sqrt{.1451 \times 26}$ = $\sqrt{3.77}$ = 1.94

3- $\sqrt{.1093 \times 26}$ = $\sqrt{2.84}$ = 1.69

4- $\sqrt{.0875 \times 26}$ = $\sqrt{2.28}$ = 1.51

5- $\sqrt{.0729 \times 26}$ = $\sqrt{1.90}$ = 1.38

6- $\sqrt{.0625 \times 26}$ = $\sqrt{1.63}$ = 1.28

7- $\sqrt{.0546 \times 26}$ = $\sqrt{1.42}$ = 1.19

8- $\sqrt{.0486 \times 26}$ = $\sqrt{1.26}$ = 1.12

9- $\sqrt{.0437 \times 26}$ = $\sqrt{1.14}$ = 1.07

NO. OF TIMES THE WORD (HOLY) "SPIRIT" IN GREEK AND ENGLISH IS USED PER BOOK OF THE N.T. (KING JAMES VERSION) STRONG'S CONCORDANCE

First Digit	Fourth Order-Theoretical Proportion	$\overline{X}$ Theoretical Population	X Actual Population	$X - \overline{X}$	ESD	(Z) $\dfrac{X - \overline{X}}{ESD}$	$(Z)^2$
1	.3010	6	10	+4	2.05	**+1.95**	3.80
2	.1761	4	5	+1	1.70	+0.59	0.35
3	.1249	2	0	-2	1.48	**-1.35**	1.82
4	.0969	2	2	0	1.32	0.00	0.00
5	.0792	2	2	0	1.21	0.00	0.00
6	.0670	1	1	0	1.12	0.00	0.00
7	.0580	1	0	-1	1.04	-0.96	0.92
8	.0512	1	0	-1	0.98	-1.02	1.04
9	.0458	1	0	-1	0.93	-1.08	1.17
Totals	1.0000	20	20			$\Sigma(Z)^2=$	**9.10**
						chi-square	**6.91**

ESD

First Digit

1- $\sqrt{.2104 \times 20}$ = $\sqrt{4.21}$ = 2.05

2- $\sqrt{.1451 \times 20}$ = $\sqrt{2.90}$ = 1.70

3- $\sqrt{.1093 \times 20}$ = $\sqrt{2.19}$ = 1.48

4- $\sqrt{.0875 \times 20}$ = $\sqrt{1.75}$ = 1.32

5- $\sqrt{.0729 \times 20}$ = $\sqrt{1.46}$ = 1.21

6- $\sqrt{.0625 \times 20}$ = $\sqrt{1.25}$ = 1.12

7- $\sqrt{.0546 \times 20}$ = $\sqrt{1.09}$ = 1.04

8- $\sqrt{.0486 \times 20}$ = $\sqrt{0.97}$ = 0.98

9- $\sqrt{.0437 \times 20}$ = $\sqrt{0.87}$ = 0.93

NO. OF TIMES THE WORD (HOLY) "GHOST" IN GREEK AND ENGLISH IS USED PER BOOK OF THE N.T. (KING JAMES VERSION) STRONG'S CONCORDANCE

First Digit	Fourth Order-Theoretical Proportion	$\overline{X}$ Theoretical Population	X Actual Population	$X - \overline{X}$	ESD	(Z) $\dfrac{X-\overline{X}}{ESD}$	$(Z)^2$
1	.3010	5	7	+2	1.84	**+1.09**	1.19
2	.1761	3	2	-1	1.52	-0.66	0.44
3	.1249	2	1	-1	1.32	-0.76	0.58
4	.0969	2	3	+1	1.18	+0.85	0.72
5	.0792	1	2	+1	1.08	+0.93	0.86
6	.0670	1	1	0	1.00	0.00	0.00
7	.0580	1	0	-1	0.93	-1.08	1.17
8	.0512	1	0	-1	0.88	-1.14	1.30
9	.0458	1	0	-1	0.84	**-1.19**	1.42
Totals	1.0000	(17)	16			$\Sigma(Z)^2 =$	**7.68**
						chi-square	**6.13**

ESD

First Digit

1- $\sqrt{.2104 \times 16}$ = $\sqrt{3.37}$ = 1.84

2- $\sqrt{.1451 \times 16}$ = $\sqrt{2.32}$ = 1.52

3- $\sqrt{.1093 \times 16}$ = $\sqrt{1.75}$ = 1.32

4- $\sqrt{.0875 \times 16}$ = $\sqrt{1.40}$ = 1.18

5- $\sqrt{.0729 \times 16}$ = $\sqrt{1.17}$ = 1.08

6- $\sqrt{.0625 \times 16}$ = $\sqrt{1.00}$ = 1.00

7- $\sqrt{.0546 \times 16}$ = $\sqrt{0.87}$ = 0.93

8- $\sqrt{.0486 \times 16}$ = $\sqrt{0.78}$ = 0.88

9- $\sqrt{.0437 \times 16}$ = $\sqrt{0.70}$ = 0.84

NO. OF TIMES THE WORD (HOLY) "SPIRIT" AND "GHOST" IN GREEK AND ENGLISH IS USED PER BOOK OF THE N.T. (KING JAMES VERSION) STRONG'S CONCORDANCE

First Digit	Fourth Order-Theoretical Proportion	$\overline{X}$ Theoretical Population	X Actual Population	$X - \overline{X}$	ESD	(Z) $\dfrac{X-\overline{X}}{ESD}$	$(Z)^2$
1	.3010	7	11	+4	2.20	**+1.82**	3.31
2	.1761	4	5	+1	1.83	+0.55	0.30
3	.1249	3	0	-3	1.58	**-1.90**	3.61
4	.0969	2	1	-1	1.42	-0.70	0.49
5	.0792	2	3	+1	1.30	+0.77	0.59
6	.0670	2	1	-1	1.20	-0.83	0.69
7	.0580	1	1	0	1.12	0.00	0.00
8	.0512	1	1	0	1.06	0.00	0.00
9	.0458	1	0	-1	1.00	-1.00	1.00
Totals	1.0000	23	23			$\sum(Z)^2=$	**9.99**
						chi-square	**8.04**

ESD

First Digit

1- $\sqrt{.2104 \times 23}$ = $\sqrt{4.84}$ = 2.20

2- $\sqrt{.1451 \times 23}$ = $\sqrt{3.34}$ = 1.83

3- $\sqrt{.1093 \times 23}$ = $\sqrt{2.51}$ = 1.58

4- $\sqrt{.0875 \times 23}$ = $\sqrt{2.01}$ = 1.42

5- $\sqrt{.0729 \times 23}$ = $\sqrt{1.68}$ = 1.30

6- $\sqrt{.0625 \times 23}$ = $\sqrt{1.44}$ = 1.20

7- $\sqrt{.0546 \times 23}$ = $\sqrt{1.26}$ = 1.12

8- $\sqrt{.0486 \times 23}$ = $\sqrt{1.12}$ = 1.06

9- $\sqrt{.0437 \times 23}$ = $\sqrt{1.01}$ = 1.00

NO. OF TIMES THAT THE COMBINATION OF THE WORDS "FATHER(S)", "JESUS" AND "SPIRIT WITH GHOST" (HOLY) ARE USED PER BOOK OF THE N.T. IN GREEK ACCORDING TO THE FIRST DIGIT COUNT

First Digit	Fourth Order-Theoretical Proportion	$\overline{X}$ Theoretical Population	X Actual Population	X - $\overline{X}$	ESD	(Z) $\dfrac{X-\overline{X}}{ESD}$	$(Z)^2$
1	.3010	22	29	+7	3.95	**+1.77**	3.31
2	.1761	13	14	+1	3.28	+0.30	0.09
3	.1249	9	6	-3	2.84	**-1.06**	1.12
4	.0969	7	6	-1	2.55	-0.39	0.15
5	.0792	6	8	+2	2.32	+0.86	0.74
6	.0670	5	3	-2	2.15	-0.93	0.86
7	.0580	4	3	-1	2.01	-0.50	0.25
8	.0512	4	2	-2	1.90	-1.05	1.10
9	.0458	3	3	0	1.80	0.00	0.00
Totals	1.0000	(73)	74			$\sum(Z)^2=$ **7.44**	
						chi-square	**6.86**

ESD

First Digit

1- $\sqrt{.2104 \times 74}$ = $\sqrt{15.57}$ = 3.95

2- $\sqrt{.1451 \times 74}$ = $\sqrt{10.74}$ = 3.28

3- $\sqrt{.1093 \times 74}$ = $\sqrt{8.09}$ = 2.84

4- $\sqrt{.0875 \times 74}$ = $\sqrt{6.48}$ = 2.55

5- $\sqrt{.0729 \times 74}$ = $\sqrt{5.39}$ = 2.32

6- $\sqrt{.0625 \times 74}$ = $\sqrt{4.63}$ = 2.15

7- $\sqrt{.0546 \times 74}$ = $\sqrt{4.04}$ = 2.01

8- $\sqrt{.0486 \times 74}$ = $\sqrt{3.60}$ = 1.90

9- $\sqrt{.0437 \times 74}$ = $\sqrt{3.23}$ = 1.80

NO. OF TIMES THAT THE COMBINATION OF THE WORDS "FATHER(S)", "JESUS" AND "SPIRIT WITH GHOST" (HOLY) ARE USED PER BOOK OF THE N.T. IN GREEK ACCORDING TO THE WORD COUNT

First Digit	Fourth Order- Theoretical Proportion	$\overline{X}$ Theoretical Population	X Actual Population	X - $\overline{X}$	ESD	(Z) $\dfrac{X - \overline{X}}{ESD}$	$(Z)^2$
1	.3010	8	9	+1	2.34	+0.43	0.18
2	.1761	5	4	-1	1.94	-1.52	0.27
3	.1249	3	5	+2	1.69	**+1.18**	1.39
4	.0969	3	1	-2	1.51	-1.32	1.74
5	.0792	2	2	0	1.38	0.00	0.00
6	.0670	2	3	+1	1.28	+0.78	0.61
7	.0580	2	0	-2	1.19	**-1.68**	2.82
8	.0512	1	2	+1	1.12	+0.89	0.79
9	.0458	1	0	-1	1.07	-0.93	0.86
Totals	1.0000	(27)	26			$\sum(Z)^2=$	**8.66**
						chi-square	**7.49**

ESD

First Digit

$$1- \sqrt{.2104 \times 26} = \sqrt{5.47} = 2.34$$

$$2- \sqrt{.1451 \times 26} = \sqrt{3.77} = 1.94$$

$$3- \sqrt{.1093 \times 26} = \sqrt{2.84} = 1.69$$

$$4- \sqrt{.0875 \times 26} = \sqrt{2.28} = 1.51$$

$$5- \sqrt{.0729 \times 26} = \sqrt{1.90} = 1.38$$

$$6- \sqrt{.0625 \times 26} = \sqrt{1.63} = 1.28$$

$$7- \sqrt{.0546 \times 26} = \sqrt{1.42} = 1.19$$

$$8- \sqrt{.0486 \times 26} = \sqrt{1.26} = 1.12$$

$$9- \sqrt{.0437 \times 26} = \sqrt{1.14} = 1.07$$

NO. OF TIMES THAT THE WORD "SAVIOUR" IN GREEK IS USED PER BOOK OF THE N.T. STRONG'S CONCORDANCE (FIRST ORDER)

First Digit	First Order-Theoretical Proportion	$\overline{X}$ Theoretical Population	X Actual Population	X - $\overline{X}$	ESD	(Z) $\frac{X-\overline{X}}{ESD}$	(Z)^2
1	.3932	4	4	0	1.47	0.00	0.00
2	.2576	2	2	0	1.31	0.00	0.00
3	.1327	1	1	0	1.02	0.00	0.00
4	.0815	1	0	-1	0.82	**-1.22**	1.49
5	.0534	0	1	+1	0.67	+1.49	2.22
6	.0358	0	1	+1	0.56	**+1.79**	3.20
7	.0235	0	0	0	0.46	0.00	0.00
8	.0146	0	0	0	0.36	0.00	0.00
9	.0077	0	0	0	0.26	0.00	0.00
Totals	1.0000	(8)	9			$\sum(Z)^2=$	**6.91**
						chi-square	**6.21**

ESD

First Digit

1- $\sqrt{.2386 \times 9}$ = $\sqrt{2.15}$ = 1.47

2- $\sqrt{.1912 \times 9}$ = $\sqrt{1.72}$ = 1.31

3- $\sqrt{.1151 \times 9}$ = $\sqrt{1.04}$ = 1.02

4- $\sqrt{.0749 \times 9}$ = $\sqrt{0.67}$ = 0.82

5- $\sqrt{.0505 \times 9}$ = $\sqrt{0.45}$ = 0.67

6- $\sqrt{.0345 \times 9}$ = $\sqrt{0.31}$ = 0.56

7- $\sqrt{.0229 \times 9}$ = $\sqrt{0.21}$ = 0.46

8- $\sqrt{.0144 \times 9}$ = $\sqrt{0.13}$ = 0.36

9- $\sqrt{.0076 \times 9}$ = $\sqrt{0.07}$ = 0.26

NO. OF TIMES THE WORD "SAVIOUR" IN GREEK IS USED PER BOOK OF THE N.T. STRONG'S CONCORDANCE (FOURTH ORDER)

First Digit	Fourth Order-Theoretical Proportion	$\overline{X}$ Theoretical Population	X Actual Population	$X - \overline{X}$	ESD	(Z) $\dfrac{X-\overline{X}}{ESD}$	$(Z)^2$
1	.3010	3	4	+1	1.37	**+0.73**	0.53
2	.1761	2	2	0	1.14	0.00	0.00
3	.1249	1	1	0	0.99	0.00	0.00
4	.0969	1	0	-1	0.89	-1.12	1.25
5	.0792	1	1	0	0.81	0.00	0.00
6	.0670	1	1	0	0.75	0.00	0.00
7	.0580	1	0	-1	0.70	**-1.43**	2.04
8	.0512	0	0	0	0.66	0.00	0.00
9	.0458	0	0	0	0.62	0.00	0.00
Totals	1.0000	(10)	9			$\sum(Z)^{2=}$	**3.82**
						chi-square	**2.33**

ESD

First Digit

$$1- \sqrt{.2104 \times 9} = \sqrt{1.89} = 1.37$$

$$2- \sqrt{.1451 \times 9} = \sqrt{1.31} = 1.14$$

$$3- \sqrt{.1093 \times 9} = \sqrt{0.98} = 0.99$$

$$4- \sqrt{.0875 \times 9} = \sqrt{0.79} = 0.89$$

$$5- \sqrt{.0729 \times 9} = \sqrt{0.66} = 0.81$$

$$6- \sqrt{.0625 \times 9} = \sqrt{0.56} = 0.75$$

$$7- \sqrt{.0546 \times 9} = \sqrt{0.49} = 0.70$$

$$8- \sqrt{.0486 \times 9} = \sqrt{0.44} = 0.66$$

$$9- \sqrt{.0437 \times 9} = \sqrt{0.39} = 0.62$$

NO. OF TIMES THAT THE WORD "GRACE" AND EQUIVALENTS ARE USED PER BOOK OF THE O.T. AND N.T. IN HEBREW AND GREEK STRONG'S CONCORDANCE

First Digit	First Order-Theoretical Proportion	$\overline{X}$ Theoretical Population	X Actual Population	X - $\overline{X}$	ESD	(Z) $\dfrac{X-\overline{X}}{ESD}$	(Z)^2
1	.3932	15	14	-1	2.97	-0.34	0.12
2	.2576	10	9	-1	2.66	-0.38	0.14
3	.1327	5	4	-1	2.06	**-0.49**	0.24
4	.0815	3	4	+1	1.66	+0.60	0.36
5	.0534	2	3	+1	1.37	**+0.73**	0.53
6	.0358	1	1	0	1.13	0.00	0.00
7	.0235	1	1	0	0.92	0.00	0.00
8	.0146	1	1	0	0.73	0.00	0.00
9	.0077	0	0	0	0.53	0.00	0.00
Totals	1.0000	(38)	37			$\sum(Z)^2 =$	**1.39**
						chi-square	**1.20**

ESD

First Digit

1- $\sqrt{.2386 \times 37}$ = $\sqrt{8.83}$ = 2.97

2- $\sqrt{.1912 \times 37}$ = $\sqrt{7.07}$ = 2.66

3- $\sqrt{.1151 \times 37}$ = $\sqrt{4.26}$ = 2.06

4- $\sqrt{.0749 \times 37}$ = $\sqrt{2.77}$ = 1.66

5- $\sqrt{.0505 \times 37}$ = $\sqrt{1.87}$ = 1.37

6- $\sqrt{.0345 \times 37}$ = $\sqrt{1.28}$ = 1.13

7- $\sqrt{.0229 \times 37}$ = $\sqrt{0.85}$ = 0.92

8- $\sqrt{.0144 \times 37}$ = $\sqrt{0.53}$ = 0.73

9- $\sqrt{.0076 \times 37}$ = $\sqrt{0.28}$ = 0.53

Please note that the last analysis included the word Grace (in Hebrew and Greek) as found in both the Old and New Testaments. So even with a random pick of common words, we see a better than perfect fit for conformity to the Law of First Digits. And, there are many, many other examples. How amazing is that.

What if we now consider a different approach and asked what is the ratio of the actual number of letters in both the Old Testament and the New Testament to the total number of First Digit Numbers in each? That is, we take the total number of actual letter (these are published statistics) and divide them by the total number of First Significant Digits found in each book based on our research.

Supernatural Ratios

> *"...Till heaven and earth pass, one jot or one title shall in no wise pass from the law, till all be fulfilled."*
> **Matthew 5:18**

An amazing "coincidence" emerges from this analysis concerning these ratios. Below is a brief summary of this incredible "coincidence".

Number of Letters per First Digit Number (First Order)

Old Testament

2,728,100 (Total Letters) / 2,305 (Total First Digit Numbers) = 1,183.56

Rounder to Whole Number → **1,184**

New Testament

838,380 (Total Letters) / 708 (Total Frist Digit Numbers) = 1,184.15

Rounded to Whole Number → **1,184**

Incredibly, the ratios are exactly the same. Some will say this is a "coincidence", but you draw your own conclusions. Obviously, I was being facetious about this being a coincidence because the probability of this occurrence happening by chance is nearly <u>zero.</u> The only logical explanation is that the underlying structure of the Bible is based on a precise order or design that follows a mathematical formula that is derived from a True Natural Scientific Law of the Universe known as the Law of First Digits. Therefore, our general hypothesis concerning the authenticity of the Bible is true with a very high probability.

Describing the DNA of Scripture

If we view the upcoming chart, we see that the DNA of the Holy Scriptures appear to be a Chaotic Array of numbers, whereas it will be shown that they are arranged in a precise order or design that follows a mathematical formula derived from a True Natural Scientific Law of the Universe known as the Law of First Digits. The grid numbers in this chart are the DNA of Scripture for the King James Version of the Holy Bible, which conform to one of God's own Natural Laws of the Universe.

The direct observation of this grid of numbers would not reveal the precise mathematical order without the assistance of the understanding of the science of modern mathematics and statistics. However, the mystery begins to unravel as shown in the subsequent chart where each line is labeled for each book of the Bible and each column is labeled for the significant digits (first order) one (1) through nine (9) with the last column representing the total for that particular line. For example, the first line is represented by the book of Genesis in the Old Testament and the total number of the significant digit ones (1) is 37; for digit two (2) it is 55, and so forth through digit nine (9) which is 0. The total of all the significant digits one (1) through nine (9) for Genesis is 170. This is repeated for every book in both the Old and New Testaments.

The vertical and horizontal columns of numbers are then totaled for both the Old Testament and the New Testament to assist you in determining what order or design exists. A summary of the population numbers for each significant digit is shown in the Appendix along with the variations of the word numbers that were actually counted. (Example: one, once, two, twain, twain, double, both, three, thrice, etc.) The total number of significant first digits in the entire Bible is 3,013—708 in the New Testament and 2,305 in the Old Testament.

37	55	21	3	6	2	43	3	0	170
75	118	30	33	24	23	14	3	0	320
32	41	5	5	4	5	45	0	0	137
153	61	19	2	40	4	32	2	2	315
18	25	10	2	0	4	11	0	1	71
45	13	9	9	7	4	15	0	5	107
18	16	7	4	5	1	9	2	0	62
2	9	0	0	0	2	1	0	0	14
25	30	21	1	10	1	7	1	0	96
21	17	21	2	2	5	5	0	1	74
43	45	18	11	12	5	9	1	0	144
17	35	15	1	5	3	8	2	1	87
8	7	27	10	7	10	8	1	1	79
17	16	16	0	17	4	14	5	0	89
2	2	5	0	0	0	3	0	0	12
5	4	1	1	0	1	1	0	1	14
4	4	1	0	0	2	4	0	0	15
9	5	8	2	0	1	7	0	0	32
8	2	0	0	0	0	2	0	0	12
2	9	4	5	0	1	5	0	0	26
17	5	1	0	0	0	1	1	0	25
4	5	0	0	0	0	0	0	0	0
16	13	4	2	3	1	3	0	0	42
8	11	3	5	1	1	3	1	0	33
0	0	0	0	0	0	0	0	0	0
67	30	19	39	9	12	17	5	0	198
7	8	13	13	0	1	6	0	0	48
1	2	0	0	0	0	0	0	0	3
0	0	0	0	0	0	0	0	0	0
4	4	11	8	0	0	1	0	0	28
1	0	0	0	0	0	0	0	0	1
0	0	3	0	0	0	0	0	0	3
0	0	0	0	0	0	0	1	1	2
0	0	0	0	0	0	0	0	0	0
0	0	0	0	0	0	0	0	0	0
1	0	0	0	0	0	0	0	0	1
2	0	0	0	0	0	0	0	0	2
9	10	1	5	0	0	5	0	0	30
4	0	0	0	0	0	0	0	0	4
53	43	14	1	12	1	10	0	0	134
32	20	7	2	3	1	9	0	0	74
43	29	12	1	9	2	8	2	1	107
33	13	4	4	4	3	0	1	0	62
15	16	17	9	2	2	8	1	0	70
20	0	0	1	0	0	0	0	0	21
32	3	3	0	1	0	0	0	0	39
3	1	4	0	1	0	0	0	0	9
7	2	1	0	0	0	0	0	0	10
14	2	0	0	0	0	0	0	0	16
4	1	0	0	0	0	0	0	0	5
1	0	0	0	0	0	0	0	0	1
2	0	0	0	0	0	0	0	0	2
2	0	0	0	0	0	0	0	0	2
5	2	1	0	0	0	0	0	0	8
0	0	0	0	0	0	0	0	0	0
1	0	0	0	0	0	0	0	0	1
0	0	0	0	0	0	0	0	0	0
5	3	2	0	0	0	1	0	0	11
3	2	1	0	0	1	0	0	0	7
0	0	0	0	0	0	0	1	0	1
3	0	0	0	0	0	0	0	0	3
2	0	4	0	0	0	0	0	0	6
0	0	0	0	0	0	0	0	0	0
0	0	0	0	0	0	0	0	0	0
0	1	0	0	0	0	0	0	0	1
17	15	11	19	3	1	53	0	0	119
978	755	374	200	187	104	369	33	13	3013

Chart of Significant First Digits per Books of the Bible

Old Testament

Book of the Holy Bible	Digit 1	Digit 2	Digit 3	Digit 4	Digit 5	Digit 6	Digit 7	Digit 8	Digit 9	Totals
Genesis	37	55	21	3	6	2	43	3	0	170
Exodus	75	118	30	33	24	23	14	3	0	320
Leviticus	32	41	5	5	4	5	45	0	0	137
Numbers	153	61	19	2	40	4	32	2	2	315
Deuteronomy	18	25	10	2	0	4	11	0	1	71
Joshua	45	13	9	9	7	4	15	0	5	107
Judges	18	16	7	4	5	1	9	2	0	62
Ruth	2	9	0	0	0	2	1	0	0	14
I Samuel	25	30	21	1	10	1	7	1	0	96
II Samuel	21	17	21	2	2	5	5	0	1	74
I Kings	43	45	18	11	12	5	9	1	0	144
II Kings	17	35	15	1	5	3	8	2	1	87
I Chronicles	8	7	27	10	7	10	8	1	1	79
II Chronicles	17	16	16	0	17	4	14	5	0	89
Ezra	2	2	5	0	0	0	3	0	0	12
Nehemiah	5	4	1	1	0	1	1	0	1	14
Esther	4	4	1	0	0	2	4	0	0	15
Job	9	5	8	2	0	1	7	0	0	32
Psalms	8	2	0	0	0	0	2	0	0	12
Proverbs	2	9	4	5	0	1	5	0	0	26
Ecclesiastes	17	5	1	0	0	0	1	1	0	25
Song of Soloman	4	5	0	0	0	0	0	0	0	9
Isaiah	16	13	4	2	3	1	3	0	0	42
Jeremiah	8	11	3	5	1	1	3	1	0	33
Lamentations	0	0	0	0	0	0	0	0	0	0
Ezekiel	67	30	19	39	9	12	17	5	0	198
Daniel	7	8	13	13	0	1	6	0	0	48
Hosea	1	2	0	0	0	0	0	0	0	3
Joel	0	0	0	0	0	0	0	0	0	0
Amos	4	4	11	8	0	0	1	0	0	28
Obadiah	1	0	0	0	0	0	0	0	0	1
Jonah	0	0	3	0	0	0	0	0	0	3
Micah	0	0	0	0	0	0	1	1	0	2
Nahum	0	0	0	0	0	0	0	0	0	0
Habakkuk	0	0	0	0	0	0	0	0	0	0
Zephaniah	1	0	0	0	0	0	0	0	0	1
Haggai	2	0	0	0	0	0	0	0	0	2
Zechariah	9	10	1	5	0	0	5	0	0	30
Malachi	4	0	0	0	0	0	0	0	0	4
O.T. Totals	682	602	293	163	152	93	280	28	12	2305
Actual Proportion	.2959	.2612	.1271	.0707	.0659	.0403	.1215	.0121	.0052	

Chart of Significant First Digits per Books of the Bible

New Testament

Book of the Holy Bible	Digit 1	Digit 2	Digit 3	Digit 4	Digit 5	Digit 6	Digit 7	Digit 8	Digit 9	Totals
Matthew	53	43	14	1	12	1	10	0	0	134
Mark	32	20	7	2	3	1	9	0	0	74
Luke	43	29	12	1	9	2	8	2	1	107
John	33	13	4	4	4	3	0	1	0	62
Acts	15	16	17	9	2	2	8	1	0	70
Romans	20	0	0	1	0	0	0	0	0	21
I Corinthians	32	3	3	0	1	0	0	0	0	39
II Corinthians	3	1	4	0	1	0	0	0	0	9
Galatians	7	2	1	0	0	0	0	0	0	10
Ephesians	14	2	0	0	0	0	0	0	0	16
Philippians	4	1	0	0	0	0	0	0	0	5
Colossians	1	0	0	0	0	0	0	0	0	1
I Thessalonians	2	0	0	0	0	0	0	0	0	2
II Thessalonians	1	0	0	0	0	0	0	0	0	1
I Timothy	5	2	1	0	0	0	0	0	0	8
II Timothy	0	0	0	0	0	0	0	0	0	0
Titus	1	0	0	0	0	0	0	0	0	1
Philemon	0	0	0	0	0	0	0	0	0	0
Hebrews	5	3	2	0	0	0	1	0	0	11
James	3	2	1	0	0	1	0	0	0	7
I Peter	0	0	0	0	0	0	0	1	0	1
II Peter	3	0	0	0	0	0	0	0	0	3
I John	2	0	4	0	0	0	0	0	0	6
II John	0	0	0	0	0	0	0	0	0	0
III John	0	0	0	0	0	0	0	0	0	0
Jude	0	1	0	0	0	0	0	0	0	1
Revelation	17	15	11	19	3	1	53	0	0	119
N.T. Totals	296	153	81	37	35	11	89	5	1	708
Actual Proportion	.4181	.2161	.1144	.0523	.0494	.0155	.1257	.0071	.0014	
Entire Bible Total	978	755	374	200	187	104	369	33	13	3013
Actual Proportion	.3246	.2506	.1241	.0664	.0621	.0345	.1225	.0110	.0043	
Theoretical Proportion	.3932	.2576	.1327	.0815	.0535	.0358	.0235	.0146	.0077	

All comparisons and analyzes of the Holy Scriptures using the Law of First Digits are based on the above two labeled charts of raw data.

Summary of other Proofs Relating to the Holy Bible

In analyzing the Bible using the precise measurements of first significant number digits, we find even more proofs of total conformity when comparing diverse books to one another. The following comparative analysis bears this out:

1. The Torah (the first five books of the Old Testament) was written by the Hand of God as dictated to Moses and is the basis for three world religions.
2. The Torah conforms to the Law of First Digits except for the number digit 7, which, as shown above, is a special exception as determined by the Torah itself and other books of the Scripture. (The number seven (7) is considered a holy number representing the Word of God, perfection and completion.)
3. The remaining books of the Old Testament conform to the Law of First Digits with the same noted exception for the number seven.
4. When item #2 is overlaid on item # 3, there is a near perfect fit.
5. When the Gospel Books (the first four books of the New Testament and Revelation) are applied to the Law of First Digits, there is a close conformity to item #2.
6. When the remaining New Testament books are analyzed in the same manner, there is close conformity to items #2, #3, and #5.

An interesting side note: The verses and chapters of the Bible are manmade constructs. The original manuscripts were not formatted but consisted of continuous text and were not formatted into chapters and verses until the 13th century. The software we used in the analysis of our modern day Bible automatically skips chapter numbers, verse numbers and page numbers.

Treating the Bible as Matter

In retrospect, we made our analysis more interesting by disregarding the actual content of the Bible, thereby eliminating all the conflict regarding theology, interpretation, inter-denominational squabbles and other religious battles. We only concerned ourselves with the clinical observations relating to the first significant digits found throughout the Bible just as we would with the universal matter analyzes shown in chapter 3. In this way we have demonstrated the first scientific proof that is outside the Bible itself—a feat no other religion or religious document can claim.

Consequently, the implications of this proof that the entire Bible conforms to one of the many natural laws of science (i.e., God's laws) and is therefore the authentic Word of God are staggering. If the entire Bible contains this outside "Signature of God" as we have demonstrated, does not this bring into question the "long suffering truths" of the Jewish religion, which lend no credence to the New Testament and believes that the Messiah has not yet come; What about the atheist and evolutionist who believe in the scientific purity of naturalism but who brush aside any talk of a Supernatural Being; the theistic evolutionist (including the Catholic Church) who believes in both evolution *and* God and wants to please everyone and everything but the truth? This realization of the absolute authentication—and by extension the truth of and the inerrancy of—the Holy Bible from outside itself provides a lofty and compelling argument which towers above the mundane arguments of mere man. <u>God is alive and He is with us in His Word.</u>

What the Distribution of Significant First Digit Numbers tells us about the Truth of the Bible.

So, what does all of this mean to each of us?

- At a minimum, the conformity of the distribution of first digit numbers to the Law of First Digits logically tells us that we may be able to trust the truth of the remaining text of Scripture with a *high level of probability*. Conversely, the non-conformity of the distribution of First Digit numbers to the Law of First Digits logically would not allow us to trust the truth of the remaining text of any alleged sacred scripture with any level of probability.

- At a maximum, the conformity of the distribution of First Digit numbers to the Law of First Digits logically tells us that we can trust the remaining text of Scripture with a *very high level of probability*. The First Digit numbers in the Scripture are equivalent to other words in Scripture. In fact, numbers in Scripture are actually designated by their numerical word representation, not their mathematical figure or symbol. Therefore, word numbers are a sampling of the total word population in Scripture.

The real question then becomes, "Is the 'word sampling' of numbers a true representation of the other words in Scripture?" We know that in statistical quality control sampling analysis, a small random sample can represent the quality of the entire population with a very high level of probability. <u>But Scripture has an additional aspect in that each word is intimately related to the words adjacent to and immediately around it.</u> In other words, if the number is true then the phrase must be true. If the phrase is true, then the sentence is true. If each sentence is true, the verse is true. If each verse is true, then the chapter is true. If each chapter is true, then the book is true. If each book is true, the testaments are true, and then the entire Scripture is therefore true.

So, the Law of First Digits tells us unequivocally that there is a very high probability that text of the Holy Scripture is true just based on the sampling probability. However, there are dozens and dozens of other comparative analyses using the Law of First Digits which dispel any chance of coincidence where the probability of any conformity is less than perfect fit.[52]

As we stated earlier, the implications of this new proof that the *entire* Scripture is the authentic Word of God are indeed staggering. For example, if this scientific proof holds—and we are confident that it will—then Judaism must now accept the fact that Jesus is the Messiah. The logic behind this statement is unassailable: those of the Jewish faith believe that only the Old Testament as the infallible Word of God; we have now proven that both the Old Testament *and* New Testaments conform to the Law of First Digits with a better than perfect fit, statistically speaking; therefore, *both* testaments of the Bible must be the true Word of God. Consequently, since the New Testament states that Jesus is the Messiah, then by definition they are forced to accept it.

<u>The True god of the Universe can now be identified. If the Scriptures are proven true, then the God to whom those Scriptures refer must be real and is therefore revealed.</u>

CHAPTER 5

Applying the Law of First Digits to Scripture of the World Religions

Although applying the Law of First Digits to only one document of Scripture—in this case the King James Version of the Holy Bible—does provide us with mathematical proof showing an unerring conformity to the Law of First Digits, it does not, in a statistical sense, provide us with a wider sample from which to compare the conformity to other religious scriptures. In this sense we can clearly draw conclusions by direct comparisons.

The different religions argue their own truth based on many factors: purported sacred scripture and teachings; other historical documents; myths; customs and verbal theology handed down over time; or simply attacking other religions by identifying perceived contradictions, mistranslations, incorrect definitions, contextual errors or finding errors of fact. With so many religious dogmas and false facades, how is one to cut through the discord and confusion to determine which religion possesses the truth.

To penetrate this fog of confusion, what is needed is a universally agreed upon *baseline or standard of truth* against which to measure the veracity, or lack thereof, of the Holy Scriptures of the various world religions. We obviously cannot use a subjective standard such as a particular religious dogma or faith as such a standard cannot be proven scientifically using the scientific method.

In this context, what would represent a consensus of opinion? It is assumed that no one can legitimately argue against any of the proven laws of natural science, i.e., the fundamental physical constants of the universe: say for example the Newtonian Constant of Gravitation (symbol G, which has a constant parameter of 6.673 x 10-11 m3 kg-1 s-2.) Everyone knows this law to be ever constant and non-changing from the beginning of the physical universe. In layman's terms, everyone knows that you can throw an object off of a building and it will fall downward at a certain accelerated rate and hit the ground at a certain velocity every time from the same height. And, it is universally accepted that this one truth of science has, of course, been proven by experiment after experiment.

In that sense, another proven true natural law of science is the Law of First Digits or Benford's law, has been fully described and explained in this book. Although only recently confirmed into this exclusive club of scientific natural laws, it has the unique quality and ability to identify the natural numbers one (1) through nine (9)—both in nature and in life happenings on earth —in a particular geometric progression or distribution. If the frequency or distribution of these significant first digit numbers as found, say in the composition of matter in nature or, as in this case, in various Holy Scriptures, does not conform to the precise percentages predicted by the law, then there is a very high probability that the substance or document is not natural and is therefore false. In other words, the numbers must conform to the Law of First Digits in order to be true.

The frequency that each first significant number appears follows a precise mathematical formula wherein each individual number bears a certain percentage of the total population every time. (For example, the first significant number digit one (1) will occur approximately 30.1% of the time as opposed to the number digit nine (9) which will occur approximately 4.5% of the time.)

Therefore, using this scientific baseline or standard represents a starting point in resolving the highly contentious issue of which religion has the truth outside of faith.

So in keeping with the theme of religious or sacred scripture analysis, and given the proof shown in the previous chapter, it would follow that if any other alleged holy scripture—be it the Koran, the Torah (Islam), the Book or Mormon, etc.—*did conform* to the Law of First Digits, as does the Bible, then our conclusion that the Bible is the sole infallible Word of God and reveals His identity would be wrong. A finding of this nature would suggest there is either (1) an anomaly in the mathematical model or the Law of First Digits is not true to itself and its unique patterns can be found in random writings.

On the other hand, if there is only One True God of the Christian religion—as we proclaim—and His Word is truth, then if follows that the alleged Holy Scriptures of the other world religions *would not conform* to the same true natural law of science known as The Law of First Digits.

Let us dive in and analyze each of the world's great religious documents and see where the chips may fall.

The Koran

The Koran (or Quran) literally meaning "the recitation", is the central religious text of Islam, which Muslims believe to be a revelation from God (*Allah*). It is widely regarded as the finest piece of literature in the Arabic language. Muslims consider the Quran to be the only book that has been protected by God from distortion or corruption. However, some significant textual variations (employing different wordings) and deficiencies in the Arabic script mean the relationship between the text of today's Quran and any original text is unclear. Qur'anic chapters are called suras and verses are called ayahs.

Muslims believe that the Koran (Quran) was verbally revealed from God to Muhammad through the angel Gabriel, gradually over a period of approximately 23 years, beginning on 22 December 609 CE, when Muhammad was 40, and concluding in 632 CE, the year of his death. Shortly after Muhammad's death, the Koran was collected by his companions using written Qur'anic materials and everything that had been memorized of the Koran.

Muslims regard the Koran as the most important miracle of Muhammad, the proof of his prophet hood and the culmination of a series of divine messages that started with the messages revealed to Adam and ended with Muhammad. The Koran assumes familiarity with major narratives recounted in the Jewish and Christian scriptures. It summarizes some, dwells at length on others and, in some cases, presents alternative accounts and interpretations of events. The Koran describes itself as a book of guidance. It sometimes offers detailed accounts of specific historical events, and it often emphasizes the moral significance of an event over its narrative sequence.

Other than the similarly of being God inspired and protected from corruption, there are clearly *major differences* in the Koran and the Bible. When we apply our software to analyze any conformity to the Law of First Digits, it is no surprise that none exists as shown in the chart and graph below.

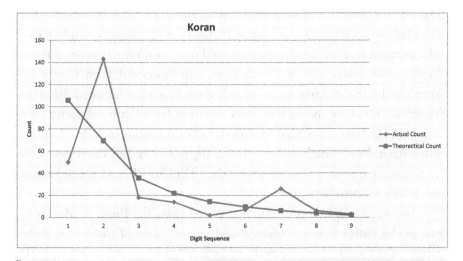

IMPORTED TEST DATA			First Digit	First Order	$\bar{X}$	X	X - $\bar{X}$	X - $\bar{X}$	ESD	(Z)	(Z)²
Koran				Theoretical Proportion	Theoretical Population	Actual Population	2 decimals	Rounded		$\dfrac{X - \bar{X}}{ESD}$	
Digit	Count	% of Total									
1	50	18.59%	1	0.3932	106	50	-55.77	-56.00	7.52	-7.44	55.41
2	143	53.16%	2	0.2576	69	143	73.71	74.00	6.25	11.84	140.30
3	18	6.69%	3	0.1327	36	18	-17.70	-18.00	5.42	-3.32	11.02
4	14	5.20%	4	0.0815	22	14	-7.92	-8.00	4.85	-1.65	2.72
5	2	0.74%	5	0.0534	14	2	-12.36	-12.00	4.43	-2.71	7.34
6	7	2.60%	6	0.0358	10	7	-2.63	-3.00	4.10	-0.73	0.54
7	26	9.67%	7*	0.0235	6	26	19.68	20.00	3.83	5.22	27.23
8	6	2.23%	8	0.0146	4	6	2.07	2.00	3.62	0.55	0.31
9	3	1.12%	9	0.0077	2	3	0.93	1.00	3.43	0.29	0.09
	269		Totals	1.0000	269	269				$\sum(Z)^{2=}$	244.95
										Chi- Square	196.4065716

Conformity is anything <8

	ESD			
	Estimated Standard Deviation			
First Digit	CONSTANT	ACTUAL POPULATION	SUM	SQ RT
1	0.2104	269	56.60	7.52
2	0.1451	269	39.03	6.25
3	0.1093	269	29.40	5.42
4	0.0875	269	23.54	4.85
5	0.0729	269	19.61	4.43
6	0.0625	269	16.81	4.10
7	0.0546	269	14.69	3.83
8	0.0486	269	13.07	3.62
9	0.0437	269	11.76	3.43

As can be seen, a Chi Square score of almost 200 is far and above any semblance of conformity and thus we conclude that the Koran is not the inspired true Word of God and is merely another religious writing by a supposed prophet.

Book of Mormon

Mormonism is the predominant religious tradition of the Latter Day Saint movement of Restorationist Christianity. This movement was founded by Joseph Smith, Jr. in the 1820s. During the 1830s and 1840s, Mormonism gradually distinguished itself from traditional Protestantism. Mormonism today represents the new, non-Protestant faith taught by Smith in the 1840s. After Smith's death, most Mormons followed Brigham Young west, calling themselves The Church of Jesus Christ of Latter Day Saints (LDS Church). Other variations of Mormonism include Mormon fundamentalism, which seeks to maintain practices and doctrines such as polygamy that were abandoned by the LDS Church, and various other small independent denominations.

The word *Mormon* is originally derived from the Book of Mormon, one of the faith's religious texts. Based on the name of that book, early followers of founder Joseph Smith, Jr. were called *Mormons*, and their faith was called *Mormonism*. The term was initially considered pejorative, but is no longer considered so by Mormons (although other terms such as Latter Day Saint, or LDS, are generally preferred).

Mormonism shares a common set of beliefs with the rest of the Latter Day Saint movement, including use of, and belief in, the Bible, as well as other religious texts including the *Book of Mormon,* and the *Doctrine and Covenants.* It also accepts the *Pearl of Great Price* as part of its scriptural canon, and has a history of teaching eternal marriage, eternal progression, and plural marriage, although the LDS Church formally abandoned the practice in 1891. Cultural Mormonism includes a lifestyle promoted by the Mormon institutions, and includes cultural Mormons who identify with the culture, but not necessarily the theology.

Let us examine the two most important documents:

A. **Book of Mormon**

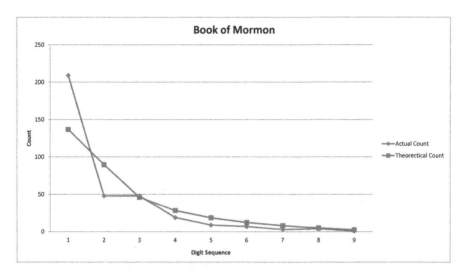

Futher Analysis on Books

		First Digit	First Order	X̄	X	X - X̄	X - X̄	ESD	(Z)	(Z)²
IMPORTED TEST DATA										
Book of Mormon				Theorectical Proportion	Theorectical Population	Actual Population	2 decimals	Rounded	X - X̄ / ESD	
Digit	Count	% of Total								
1	209	60.06%	1	0.3932	137	209	72.17	72.00	9.11	7.90	62.43
2	48	13.79%	2	0.2576	90	48	-41.64	-42.00	8.16	-5.15	26.51
3	48	13.79%	3	0.1327	46	48	1.82	2.00	6.33	0.32	0.10
4	19	5.46%	4	0.0815	28	19	-9.36	-9.00	5.11	-1.76	3.11
5	9	2.59%	5	0.0534	19	9	-9.58	-10.00	4.19	-2.39	5.69
6	7	2.01%	6	0.0358	12	7	-5.46	-5.00	3.46	-1.44	2.08
7	3	0.86%	7	0.0235	8	3	-5.18	-5.00	2.82	-1.77	3.14
8	4	1.15%	8	0.0146	5	4	-1.08	-1.00	2.24	-0.45	0.20
9	1	0.29%	9	0.0077	3	1	-1.68	-2.00	1.63	-1.23	1.51
	348		Totals	1.0000	348	348			Σ(Z)² =	104.77

need to import directly from program

| | | | Chi- Square | 72.64008956 |

 Conformity is anything <8

	ESD			
	Estimated Standard Deviation			
First Digit	CONSTANT	ACTUAL POPULATION	SUM	SQ RT
1	0.2386	348	83.03	9.11
2	0.1912	348	66.54	8.16
3	0.1151	348	40.05	6.33
4	0.0749	348	26.07	5.11
5	0.0505	348	17.57	4.19
6	0.0345	348	12.01	3.46
7	0.0229	348	7.97	2.82
8	0.0144	348	5.01	2.24
9	0.0076	348	2.64	1.63

Here again, we can see that the Book of Mormon is far from conformity with a Chi Square score of 72.64, a far cry from any acceptable statistical deviation.

B. **Doctrine and Covenants**

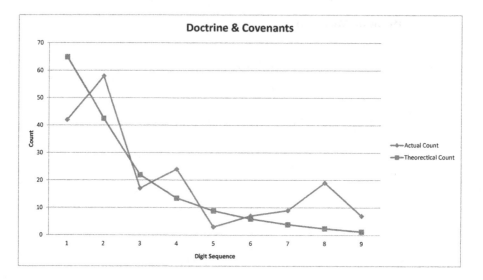

Doctrine & Covenants

Further Analysis on Books

IMPORTED TEST DATA			First Digit	First Order	X̄	X	X - X̄	X - X̄	ESD	(Z)	(Z)²
Doctrine & Covenants					Theorectical	Theorectical	Actual	2 decimals	Rounded	X - X̄	
		% of			Proportion	Population	Poplulation			ESD	
Digit	Count	Total									
1	42	22.58%	1		0.3932	65	42	-22.88	-23.00	5.89	-3.90	15.24
2	58	31.18%	2		0.2576	43	58	15.50	15.00	4.89	3.07	9.40
3	17	9.14%	3		0.1327	22	17	-4.90	-5.00	4.25	-1.18	1.39
4	24	12.90%	4		0.0815	13	24	10.55	11.00	3.80	2.89	8.38
5	3	1.61%	5		0.0534	9	3	-5.81	-6.00	3.47	-1.73	2.99
6	7	3.76%	6		0.0358	6	7	1.09	1.00	3.21	0.31	0.10
7	9	4.84%	7		0.0235	4	9	5.12	5.00	3.00	1.67	2.78
8	19	10.22%	8		0.0146	2	4	1.59	2.00	2.83	0.71	0.50
9	7	3.76%	9		0.0077	1	1	-0.27	0.00	2.69	0.00	0.00
	186		Totals		1.0000	165	165			$\sum(Z)^2 =$	40.77

need to import directly from program

Chi- Square | 35.95011287

	ESD			
	Estimated Standard Deviation			
First Digit	CONSTANT	ACTUAL POPULATION	SUM	SQ RT
1	0.2104	165	34.72	5.89
2	0.1451	165	23.94	4.89
3	0.1093	165	18.03	4.25
4	0.0875	165	14.44	3.80
5	0.0729	165	12.03	3.47
6	0.0625	165	10.31	3.21
7	0.0546	165	9.01	3.00
8	0.0486	165	8.02	2.83
9	0.0437	165	7.21	2.69

Conformity is anything <8

Although a slightly better score of 35.95, the Doctrine and Covenants scripture falls considerably short in following the Law of First Digits.

C. **Pearl of Great Price**

> The Pearl of Great Price is a selection of choice materials touching many significant aspects of the faith and doctrine of The Church of Jesus Christ of Latter-day Saints. These items were translated and produced by the Prophet Joseph Smith, and most were published in the Church periodicals of his day. Since several revisions, additions and deletions have been ongoing since 1880, there will be no need to include these materials in our analysis. [53]

Apocrypha Books

The Apocrypha is a selection of books which were published in the original 1611 King James Bible. These apocryphal books were positioned between the Old and New Testament (it also contained maps and genealogies). The Apocrypha was a part of the KJV of the Bible for 274 years until being removed in 1885 A.D. A portion of these books were called deuterocanonical books by some entities, such as the Catholic Church, and are still included as part of their Old Testament.

Many claim the Apocrypha should never have been included in the first place, raising doubt about its validity and believing it was not God inspired (for instance, a reference about magic seems inconsistent with the rest of the Bible: (Tobit chapter 6, verses 58). Others believe it is valid and that it should never have been removed—that it was considered part of the Bible for nearly 2,000 years before it was recently removed a little more than 100 years ago. Some say it was removed because of not finding the books in the original Hebrew manuscripts. Others claim it was not removed by the church, but by printers to cut costs in distributing Bibles in the United States. Both sides tend to cite the same verses that warn against adding or subtracting from the Bible: Revelation 22:18. The word 'Apocrypha' means 'hidden.' Fragments of Dead Sea Scrolls dating back prior to 70 A.D. contain parts of the Apocrypha books in Hebrew, including Sirach and Tobit.

Keep this in mind when reading the following apocryphal books: Martin Luther said, "Apocrypha—that is, books which are not regarded as equal to the Holy Scriptures, and yet are profitable and good to read."

- Esdras
- 2 Esdras
- Tobit
- Judith
- Additions to Esther
- Wisdom of Solomon
- Ecclesiasticus
- Baruch
- Letter of Jeremiah
- Prayer of Azariah
- Susanna
- Bel and the Dragon
- Prayer of Manasseh
- 1 Maccabees
- 2 Maccabees

"The Jewish canon, or the Hebrew Bible, was universally received, while the Apocrypha added to the Greek version of the Septuagint were only in a general way accounted as books suitable for church reading, and thus as a middle class between canonical and strictly apocryphal (pseudonymous) writings. And justly so; for those books, while they have great historical value, and fill the gap between the Old Testament and the New, all originated after the cessation of prophecy, and they cannot therefore be regarded as inspired, nor are they ever cited by Christ or the apostles."

There are many reasons why the Apocrypha is not inspired but chief among them are the following:

1. The Roman Catholic Church did not officially canonize the Apocrypha until the Council of Trent (1546 AD). This was in part because the Apocrypha contained material which supported certain Catholic doctrines, such as purgatory, praying for the dead, and the treasury of merit.
2. Not one of them is in the Hebrew language, which was solely used by the inspired historians and poets of the Old Testament.
3. Not one of the writers lays any claim to inspiration.
4. These books were never acknowledged as sacred Scriptures by the Jewish Church, and therefore were never sanctioned by our Lord.
5. They were not allowed a place among the sacred books, during the first four centuries of the Christian Church.

6. They contain fabulous statements that contradict not only the canonical Scriptures but themselves; as when, in the two Books of Maccabees, Antiochus Epiphanes is made to die three different deaths in as many different places.

7. The Apocrypha inculcates doctrines at variance with the Bible, such as prayers for the dead and sinless perfection.

Is the Apocrypha Inspired and does it Belong in the Bible?

For our purposes, let us consider the subject of the Catholic Apocrypha, for which they make such great claims; 2 Macc 12:38-46 seems to be the principal reason they cling to the Apocrypha. There is no other doctrine that depends so heavily upon support in the Apocrypha. It would appear that their defense of the Apocrypha is only because of the passage and their claims about its teachings.

The Catholics have 46 Old Testament books rather than the 39 found in the King James Bibles. However, they have added much more material to other books which does not appear under separate titles. That material follows: The Rest of Esther added to Esther; The Song of the Three Holy Children, The History of Susanna, Bel and the Dragon added to Daniel; Baruch; 1 and 2 Maccabees; Tobias; Judith; Ecclesiasticus; and the Wisdom of Sirach.

The only powerful support for these books is that they appear in the Septuagint version. However, in many of our Bibles there is much extraneous material that is uninspired, including history, poetry, maps, dictionaries, and other information. This may be the reason for the appearance of this material in the Septuagint. The important point is that the Apocrypha was not in the Hebrew canon.

There are reputed to be 263 quotations and 370 allusions to the Old Testament found in the New Testament and not one of them refers to the Apocryphal.

The usual division of the Old Testament by the Jews was a total of 24 books: The Books of Moses, The Late Prophets, and the Hagiographa. These 24 books contain all the material in our numbering of 39. Josephus spoke concerning the canon, but his book division combined Ruth-Judges and Lamentation-Jeremiah for a total of 22 books rather than 24.

"For we have not an innumerable multitude of books among us, only 22 books, which contain the records of all the past times; which are justly believed to be divine;... It is true, our history hath been written since Artaxerxes very particularly, but hath not been esteemed of the like authority with the former by our forefathers;...and how firmly we have given credit to these books of our own nation is evident by what we do; for during so many ages as have already passed, no one has been so bold as either to add anything to them, or to make any change in them." (Flavius Josephus against Apion Book 1, Section 8).

Plainly Josephus distinguishes between those books written before and after Artaxerxes. This eliminates most of the Apocrypha, especially the Maccabees.

The Apocrypha itself denies all notion of inspiration. Referring to the events in the Maccabees the author makes these statements:

"...all such things as have been comprised in 5 books by Jason of Cyrene, we have attempted to abridge in one book. For considering the difficulty that they find that desire to undertake the narrations of histories, because of the multitude of the matter, we have taken care for those indeed that are willing to read,...And as to ourselves indeed, in undertaking this work of abridging, we have taken in hand no easy task, yea, rather a business full of watching and sweat... Leaving to the authors the exact handling of every particular, and as for ourselves. according to the plan proposed, studying to brief... For to collect all that is known, to put the discourse in order, and curiously to discuss every particular point, is the duty of the author of a history. But to pursue brevity of speech and to avoid nice declarations of things, is to be granted to him that maketh an abridgement." (2 Maccabees 2: 24-32).

"...I will also here make an end of my narration. Which if I have done well, and as it becometh the history, it is what

I desired; but if not so perfectly, it must be pardoned me. For as it is hurtful to drink always wine, or always water, but pleasant to use sometimes the one, and sometimes the other, so if the speech be always nicely framed, it will not be grateful to the readers..." 12 Maccabees 15: 39-40).

This forms a bizarre contrast with passages in the New Testament:

"Take no thought how or what ye shall speak: for it shall be given you in that same hour what ye shall speak. For it is not ye that speak, but the spirit of your Father which speaketh in you." (Matthew 10: 19-20).

"Now we have received, not the spirit of the world but the spirit which is of God: that we might know the things that are freely given to us of God. Which things also we speak, not in words which man's wisdom teacheth, but which the Holy Ghost teacheth" (1 Corinthians 2: 12-131.

What are the Catholic arguments for the Apocrypha?

The Catholics argue that:

- The early Christians quote from the Apocrypha, which proves it belongs in the Bible. This is refuted because early Christians quoted from all kinds of uninspired writings other than the Apocrypha. Why do Catholics not include these in their Bibles?
- The Apocrypha were included in the Septuagint. This is refuted because the Jews never accepted the Apocrypha as part of the Old Testament canon.
- The Church Councils at Hippo (393) and Carthage (397, 419) listed the Apocrypha as Scripture. Since these same councils also finalized the 66 canonical books which all Christians accept, they must accept them all. This is false because the canon of the New Testament was set from the first century. It is Catholic myth that Catholics gave the world the Bible!

The New Testament never quotes from the any of the apocryphal books written between 400 - 200 BC. What is significant here is that NONE of the books within the "apocryphal collection" are ever quoted. So the Catholic argument that "the apocryphal books cannot be rejected as uninspired on the basis that they are never quoted from in the New Testament because Ezra, Nehemiah, Esther, Ecclesiastes, Song of Solomon are also never quoted in the New Testament, and we all accept them as inspired." The rebuttal to this Catholic argument is that "Ezra, Nehemiah, Esther" were always included in the "history collection" of Jewish books and "Ecclesiastes, Song of Solomon" were always included in the "poetry collection". By quoting one book from the collection, it verifies the entire collection. None of the apocryphal books were ever quoted in the New Testament. Not even once! This proves the Catholic and Orthodox apologists wrong when they try to defend the Apocrypha in the Bible.[54]

The bottom line analysis is that the Apocrypha does not belong in the Bible because it is not inspired as can also be seen in the following comparison graph. In the interest of brevity, we will use a composite data set of these books for analysis.

Chart Data
Apocrapha Comparison

Theoretical	First Digits	106	69	36	22	14	10	6	4	2
Koran	Count	50	143	18	14	2	7	26	6	3
Apocrapha	Count	40	80	27.5	12	9.5	8	16	4	2

Clearly, the Apocrypha books, as compared to the Koran and the Law of First Digits, do not measure up based on the above graph.

Another set of extra-biblical gospels and epistles were called *The Suppressed Gospels and Epistles of the Original New testament of Jesus the Christ.* These included other portions of the ancient Holy Scriptures, now extant, attributed to His apostles and their disciples, and venerated by the Primitive Christian Churches during the first four centuries. Later, after violent controversy, were forbidden by the bishops of the Nicene Council under Emperor Constantine and omitted from the Catholics and Protestant editions of the New Testament by it compilers.

A complete listing of these forbidden books is shown below:

Mary	Protevangelion	I. Infancy	II. Infancy
Nicodemus	Christ and Abgarus	Laodiceans	Paul and Seneca
Acts of Paul and Thecla	I. Clement	II. Clement	Barnabas
Ephesians	Magnesians	Trallians	Romans Philadelphians
Smyrnaeans	Polycarp	Philippians	Hermas—Visions
Hermas-- Commands	Hermas-- Similitudes		

In our research, all of these books were found in a single compilation so our analysis encompasses all of these. The graph and chart below tells the story:

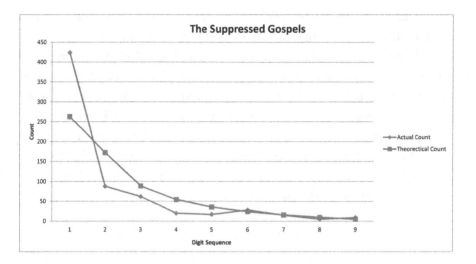

The Suppressed Gospels

Further Analysis on Books

IMPORTED TEST DATA			First Digit	First Order	X̄	X	X - X̄	X - X̄	ESD	(Z)	(Z)²
The Suppressed Gospels					Theoretical Proportion	Theoretical Population	Actual Population	2 decimals	Rounded		X - X̄ / ESD	
Digit	Count	% of Total										
1	424	63.47%	1		0.3932	263	424	161.34	161.00	11.86	13.58	184.43
2	88	13.17%	2		0.2576	172	88	-84.08	-84.00	9.85	-8.53	72.80
3	62	9.28%	3		0.1327	89	62	-26.64	-27.00	8.54	-3.16	9.98
4	20	2.99%	4		0.0815	54	20	-34.44	-34.00	7.65	-4.45	19.78
5	17	2.54%	5		0.0534	36	17	-18.67	-19.00	6.98	-2.72	7.41
6	28	4.19%	6		0.0358	24	28	4.09	4.00	6.46	0.62	0.38
7	15	2.25%	7		0.0235	16	15	-0.70	-1.00	6.04	-0.17	0.03
8	5	0.75%	8		0.0146	10	5	-4.75	-5.00	5.70	-0.88	0.77
9	9	1.35%	9		0.0077	5	9	3.86	4.00	5.40	0.74	0.55
	668		Totals		1.0000	668	668				$\sum(Z)^2 =$	296.13

need to import directly from program

		Chi- Square	185.6769062

Conformity is anything <8

	E S D Estimated Standard Deviation			
First Digit	CONSTANT	ACTUAL POPULATION	SUM	SQRT
1	0.2104	668	140.55	11.86
2	0.1451	668	96.93	9.85
3	0.1093	668	73.01	8.54
4	0.0875	668	58.45	7.65
5	0.0729	668	48.70	6.98
6	0.0625	668	41.75	6.46
7	0.0546	668	36.47	6.04
8	0.0486	668	32.46	5.70
9	0.0437	668	29.19	5.40

Not surprisingly, the aggregate score for all of these suppressed or forbidden gospels came in extremely high at 185.67—not even close.

The Book of Jasher

The Book of Jasher might be considered an exception, as one of the gnostic gospels, since it is referred to in Joshua and Second Samuel in the King James Bible:

"Is not this written in the Book of Jasher?"--Joshua, 10: 13.
"Behold it is written in the Book of Jasher."--II. Samuel, 1: 18

Also known as the "Book of the Upright One" in the Greek Septuagint and the "Book of the Just Ones" in the Latin Vulgate, the Book of Jasher was probably a collection or compilation of ancient Hebrew songs and poems praising the heroes of Israel and their exploits in battle. The Book of Jasher is referenced in Joshua 10:12-13 when the Lord stopped the sun in the middle of the day during the battle of Beth Horon. It is also mentioned in 2 Samuel 1:18-27 as containing the Song or Lament of the Bow, that mournful funeral song which David composed at the time of the death of Saul and Jonathan.

The question is, if the Book of Jasher is mentioned in the Bible, why was it left out of the canon of Scripture? We know that God directed the authors of the Scriptures to use passages from many and various extra-biblical sources in composing His Word. The passage recorded in Joshua 10:13 is a good example. In recording this battle, Joshua included passages from the Book of Jasher not because it was his only source of what occurred; rather, he was stating, in effect, "If you don't believe what I'm saying, then go read it in the Book of Jasher. Even that book has a record of this event."

There are other Hebrew works that are mentioned in the Bible that God directed the authors to use. Some of these include the Book of the Wars of the Lord (Numbers 21:14), the Book of Samuel the Seer, the Book of Nathan the Prophet, and the Book of Gad the Seer (1 Chronicles 29:29). Also, there are the Acts of Rehoboam and the Chronicles of the Kings of Judah (1 Kings 14:29). We also know that Solomon composed more than a thousand songs (1 Kings 4:32), yet only two are preserved in the book of Psalms (72 and 127). Writing under the inspiration of the Holy Spirit in the New Testament, Paul included a quotation from the Cretan poet

Epimenides (Titus 1:12) and quoted from the poets Epimenides and Aratus in his speech at Athens (Acts 17:28).

The point is that the divine Author of the Bible used materials chosen from many different sources, fitting them into His grand design for the Scriptures. We must understand that history as recorded in the Bible did not occur in isolation. The people mentioned in the Bible interacted with other people. For example, though the Bible is clear that there is only one God, the Bible mentions a number of the gods people worshipped both within Israel and in the nations around. Similarly, as in Acts 17:28 and Titus 1:12, we sometimes find secular writers being quoted. This doesn't mean that these quoted writers were inspired. It simply means they happened to say something that was useful in making a point.

There is a book called "The Book of Jasher" today, although it is not the same book as mentioned in the Old Testament. It is an eighteenth-century forgery that alleges to be a translation of the "lost" Book of Jasher by Alcuin, an eighth-century English scholar. There is also a more recent book titled "The Book of Jashar" by science fiction and fantasy writer Benjamin Rosenbaum. This book is a complete work of fiction.

Another book by this same name, called by many "Pseudo-Jasher," while written in Hebrew, is also not the "Book of Jasher" mentioned in Scripture. It is a book of Jewish legends from the creation to the conquest of Canaan under Joshua, but scholars hold that it did not exist before A.D. 1625. In addition, there are several other theological works by Jewish rabbis and scholars called "Sefer ha Yashar," but none of these claim to be the original Book of Jasher.

In the end, we must conclude that the Book of Jasher mentioned in the Bible was lost and has not survived to modern times. All we really know about it is found in the two Scripture quotations mentioned earlier. The other books by that title are mere fictions or Jewish moral treatises.[55]

There is also another spurious Book of Jasher, published 1750, in which Jasher is treated as the name of the author. The text covers much of the same ground as the traditional Mosaic books of the Bible, from the creation of the world to the death of Moses, albeit with several minor variations.

Although not the original book mentioned in the bible, and not mentioned in the two lists above, we thought it would be interesting to analyze anyway since the Bible does reference the name in the verses above. In comparing the frequency of the first significant digits to that of Benford's law we find a surprising result:

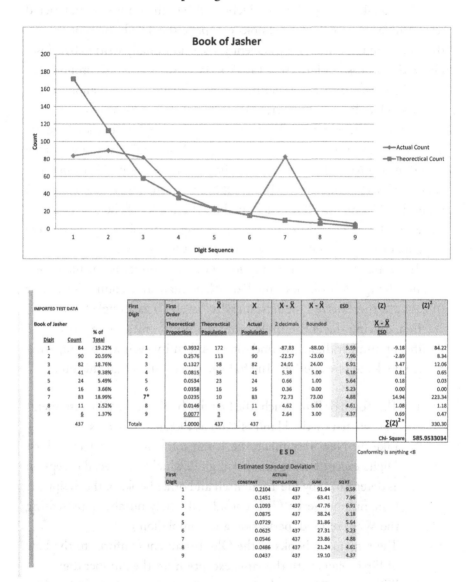

As far as conformity, Jasher is way out of the ballpark with a Chi Square score of over 585; however, the interesting part is the striking anomaly for the number seven (7), just as we found in our multiple analyzes of the Bible (See Chapter 4).

The Tanakh

The Tanakh or Tanak is the Hebrew Bible, the quintessential sacred text of Judaism. The first five books comprise the Torah (or Pentateuch), the core sacred writings of the ancient Jews, traditionally written by Moses under divine inspiration. The Tanakh (Hebrew: תַּ_נָ_ךְ, pronounced [taˈnaχ] or [təˈnax]; also Tenakh, Tenak, Tanach) is the canon of the Hebrew Bible. It is also known as the Masoretic Text or Miqra.

Tanakh is an acronym of the first Hebrew letter of each of the Masoretic Text's three traditional subdivisions: Torah ("Teaching", also known as the Five Books of Moses), Nevi'im ("Prophets") and Ketuvim ("Writings")—hence TaNaKh. The name "Miqra" (מקרא) meaning "that which is read", is another Hebrew word for the Tanakh. The books of the Tanakh were passed on by each generation, and according to rabbinic tradition were accompanied by an oral tradition, called the Oral Torah.

The Tanakh consists of twenty-four books: it counts as one book each Samuel, Kings, Chronicles and Ezra-Nehemiah and counts Trei Asar (רשעיAu רת, the Twelve Prophets; literally "twelve") as a single book.

In analyzing the entire Bible using the precise measurements of first significant number digits, we find total conformity even when comparing diverse books to one another. The following six results bear this out:

1. The Torah or Pentateuch (the first five books of the Old Testament) was written by the Hand of God as dictated to Moses.
2. Like the New Testament, the Torah conforms to the Law of First Digits except for the number digit 7, which is a special exception as determined by the Torah itself and other books of the Scripture. (The number seven (7) is considered a holy number representing the Word of God, perfection and completion.)
3. The remaining books of the Old Testament conform to the Law of First Digits with the same exception for the number digit 7.
4. When item #2 is overlaid on item # 3, there is a near perfect fit.
5. When the Gospel Books (the first four books of the New Testament and Revelation) are applied to the Law of First Digits, there is a close conformity to item #2.

6. When the remaining New Testament books are analyzed in the same manner, there is close conformity to items #2, #3, and #5.

Eastern Religions

The basic difference between Western Religions—Christianity, Judaism and Islam—and Eastern religions, such as Hinduism and Buddhism, is that of the emphasis on history. Western religions are very concerned with history: they have founders and see their history as God's own doing. They have a continuity of their scared texts and claim they are inspired by God. This strong emphasis on events differs sharply from Eastern religions where the emphasis is on the consciousness of the individual. They have a different approach to history as well as to science.

For example, Hinduism has no founder and no prophet. It has no particular ecclesiastical or institutional structure, nor set creed. The emphasis is on the way of living rather than on a way of thought. As Radhakrishnan, a former president of India once remarked: 'Hinduism is more a culture than a creed'.[56]

Likewise, Buddhist sacred texts are thought of as guides on the path to truth, not truth itself, whereas in the monotheistic religions, the Bible, Koran and other sacred books are considered the revealed truth of God.

Consequently, these Eastern religions— and there are many—are outside our comparative analysis as their sacred texts are self-defining as not claiming to be the infallible word of God.

CHAPTER 6

Applying the Law of First Digits to Non-Biblical and Non-Religious Documents

In this chapter, we will continue our application of the Law of First Digits to non-Biblical and non-religious writings to see how these results compare overall. At this early point in our research, we are confident in saying that conformity (or non-conformity) with the Law of First Digits is definitive as to truth or falsity of a given document. We now know that the Law of First Digits reveals a consistent pattern such that a document can be exposed as being either true or false.

Let us take a look at a few of the world's most famous and acclaimed books— everything from <u>Pride and Prejudice</u> to <u>Don Quixote</u> to <u>Plato's Republic</u>, <u>War and Peace</u>, <u>Democracy in America,</u> etc.

Just for fun, let's start with Plato's Republic and see what happens.

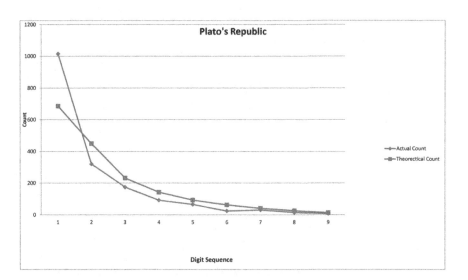

Here we have a Chi Square score of over 268. If our prior analysis holds true, then this non-conformity does not equal the truth.

What about Tolstoy's War and Peace?

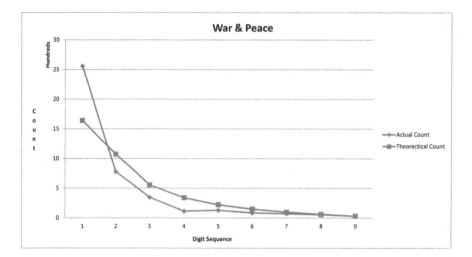

IMPORTED TEST DATA			First Digit	First Order	X̎	X	X - X̎	X - X̎	ESD	(Z)	(Z)²
War & Peace		% of		Theorectical Proportion	Theorectical Poplulation	Actual Poplulation	2 decimals	Rounded		**X - X̎** / **ESD**	
Digit	Count	Total									
1	2558	61.34%	1	0.3932	1640	2558	918.36	918.00	29.62	30.99	960.51
2	776	18.61%	2	0.2576	1074	776	-298.19	-298.00	24.60	-12.11	146.77
3	345	8.27%	3	0.1327	553	345	-208.36	-208.00	21.35	-9.74	94.92
4	114	2.73%	4	0.0815	340	114	-225.86	-226.00	19.10	-11.83	139.98
5	129	3.09%	5	0.0534	223	129	-93.68	-94.00	17.44	-5.39	29.07
6	86	2.06%	6	0.0358	149	86	-63.29	-63.00	16.14	-3.90	15.23
7	72	1.73%	7	0.0235	98	72	-26.00	-26.00	15.09	-1.72	2.97
8	58	1.39%	8	0.0146	61	58	-2.88	-3.00	14.24	-0.21	0.04
9	32	0.77%	9	0.0077	32	32	-0.11	0.00	13.50	0.00	0.00
	4170		Totals	1.0000	4170	4170				Σ(Z)² =	1389.49

need to import directly from program

Chi- Square			898.4234287
Conformity is anything <8			

		ESD Estimated Standard Deviation		
First Digit			ACTUAL	
	CONSTANT	POPULATION	SUM	SQ RT
1	0.2104	4170	877.37	29.62
2	0.1451	4170	605.07	24.60
3	0.1093	4170	455.78	21.35
4	0.0875	4170	364.88	19.10
5	0.0729	4170	303.99	17.44
6	0.0625	4170	260.63	16.14
7	0.0546	4170	227.68	15.09
8	0.0486	4170	202.66	14.24
9	0.0437	4170	182.23	13.50

As you can see there is an unbelievably high score of 898. What does this say about the book?

What about Alexis de Tocqueville's famous book, Democracy in America

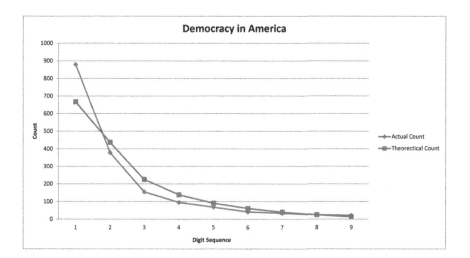

IMPORTED TEST DATA			First Digit	First Order	X̄	X	X - X̄	X - X̄	ESD	(Z)	(Z)²
Democracy in America					Theorectical Proportion	Theorectical Population	Actual Population	2 decimals	Rounded		
		% of								X - X̄	
Digit	Count	Total								ESD	
1	879	51.86%	1		0.3932	666	879	212.53	213.00	18.88	11.28	127.22
2	378	22.30%	2		0.2576	437	378	-58.63	-59.00	15.68	-3.76	14.15
3	154	9.09%	3		0.1327	225	154	-70.93	-71.00	13.61	-5.22	27.21
4	95	5.60%	4		0.0815	138	95	-43.14	-43.00	12.18	-3.53	12.47
5	68	4.01%	5		0.0534	91	68	-22.51	-23.00	11.12	-2.07	4.28
6	41	2.42%	6		0.0358	61	41	-19.68	-20.00	10.29	-1.94	3.78
7	34	2.01%	7		0.0235	40	34	-5.83	-6.00	9.62	-0.62	0.39
8	25	1.47%	8		0.0146	25	25	0.25	0.00	9.08	0.00	0.00
9	21	1.24%	9		0.0077	13	21	7.95	8.00	8.61	0.93	0.86
	1695		Totals		1.0000	1695	1695				∑(Z)² =	190.36

Chi- Square		130.085806
Conformity is anything <8		

ESD Estimated Standard Deviation				
First Digit		ACTUAL		
	CONSTANT	POPULATION	SUM	SQ RT
1	0.2104	1695	356.63	18.88
2	0.1451	1695	245.94	15.68
3	0.1093	1695	185.26	13.61
4	0.0875	1695	148.31	12.18
5	0.0729	1695	123.57	11.12
6	0.0625	1695	105.94	10.29
7	0.0546	1695	92.55	9.62
8	0.0486	1695	82.38	9.08
9	0.0437	1695	74.07	8.61

Not any better—a score of 130 does not conform to the natural order of truth.

Let's try another classic like Don Quixote:

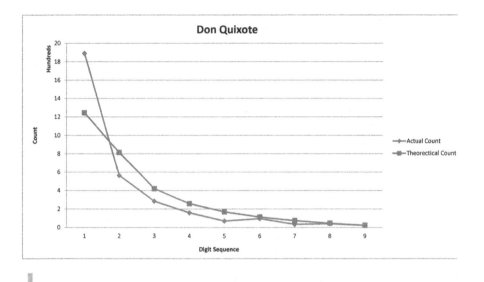

IMPORTED TEST DATA			First Digit	First Order	X̄	X	X - X̄	X - X̄	ESD	(Z)	(Z)²
Don Quixote					Theorectical Proportion	Theorectical Population	Actual Population	2 decimals	Rounded	X - X̄	
		% of								ESD	
Digit	Count	Total									
1	1890	59.72%	1	0.3932	1244	1890	645.52	646.00	25.81	25.03	626.68
2	565	17.85%	2	0.2576	815	565	-250.30	-250.00	21.43	-11.67	136.09
3	284	8.97%	3	0.1327	420	284	-136.00	-136.00	18.60	-7.31	53.47
4	160	5.06%	4	0.0815	258	160	-97.95	-98.00	16.64	-5.89	34.68
5	70	2.21%	5	0.0534	169	70	-99.01	-99.00	15.19	-6.52	42.48
6	96	3.03%	6	0.0358	113	96	-17.31	-17.00	14.06	-1.21	1.46
7	35	1.11%	7	0.0235	74	35	-39.38	-39.00	13.15	-2.97	8.80
8	41	1.30%	8	0.0146	46	41	-5.21	-5.00	12.40	-0.40	0.16
9	24	0.76%	9	0.0077	24	24	-0.37	0.00	11.76	0.00	0.00
	3165		Totals	1.0000	3165	3165				∑(Z)² =	903.82

need to import directly from program

Chi- Square: 574.7952982

Conformity is anything <8

	ESD Estimated Standard Deviation			
First Digit	CONSTANT	ACTUAL POPULATION	SUM	SQ RT
1	0.2104	3165	665.92	25.81
2	0.1451	3165	459.24	21.43
3	0.1093	3165	345.93	18.60
4	0.0875	3165	276.94	16.64
5	0.0729	3165	230.73	15.19
6	0.0625	3165	197.81	14.06
7	0.0546	3165	172.81	13.15
8	0.0486	3165	153.82	12.40
9	0.0437	3165	138.31	11.76

Wow! Another high score: 574. It appears that celebrity status does not guarantee the truth.

We now turn our attention to more modern day books of renown. Since we explored religious documents in the previous chapter, why not analyze the recent blockbuster of The Di Vinci Code by David Brown.

The Da Vinci Code

As you know by now, early Church leaders denounced the Gnostic writings as spurious and heretical. Yet modern biblical critics, along with revisionist theologians, creative writers and mystical New Agers, have resurrected these "alternative" gospels and present them as equally credible as canonical Scripture. Dan Brown, author of the highly popular and widely read fictional novel The Da Vinci Code, draws heavily on the heretical ideas of Gnostic writings, as well as on occult, pagan goddess worship and mysticism. In his novel, he "makes the case that Mary Magdalene was... a strong independent figure, patron of Jesus, and cofounder of his movement, his only believer in his greatest hour of need, author of her own Gospel, *his romantic partner, and the mother of his child.* This blending of fact and fiction created a firestorm among true believers who consider the Bible the infallible Word of God with the contingent belief that the Lost Books of the Bible (the Gnostics) were intentionally left out of the Holy Scriptures since they were not considered as inspired writings from God. To the millions of women who feel slighted, discriminated against, or unwelcome in churches of some faiths today, the novel is a chance to see early religious history in an entirely different light. Aside from its highly popular entertainment value, The Da Vinci Code presented a startlingly different view of the powerful role of women in the birth of Christianity. However, in the more secular circles, these themes have become mainstream such as at Harvard's divinity school and other intellectual centers".[57]

When Dan Brown makes his leading characters say, "Almost everything our fathers taught us about Christ is false" and, "The Bible is a product of man, my dear, not God," he is promoting an agenda and world view that seeks to undermine and discredit the Bible, and the Jesus Christ of the Bible. Though the plot of The Da Vinci Code appears to "advocate a courageous search for truth at any price, its real goal is to undermine one of the fundamental characteristics of the Christian faith—the belief that the original message of the Gospel, enshrined in the Bible, is the unique, inspired word of God".[58] The real danger of books like The Da Vinci Code comes from doubts planted in the minds of people who lack historical and biblical knowledge. For such people, the fiction of apocryphal writings can appear to be fact, which leads to deception about the true nature of inspired Scripture. One of the primary reasons for public declarations about what books comprised the canons of the Old and New Testaments was to clearly distinguish between inspired books and the false and misleading writings of the Gnostics.

However, in terms of Biblical accuracy, let us posit a theory based on our scientific analysis that exposes the master deception of what is presented as the *Holy Grail* in the Da Vinci Code and in popular culture.

Master Deception

Dan Brown has written his book as a novel but he claims that it is written with facts that reveal hidden truths with historical accuracy.

The theme of the entire book has to do with the search and subsequent finding and identification of the Holy Grail. In the course of the narrative, it was discovered that the Holy Grail is not a thing—a chalice as commonly thought—but in fact is a *person*. This person is represented by a symbol that was used throughout history in several ways. The symbol is a "vee," (pronounced like the letter "V") which is also referred to as a "chalice":

Hence the confusion. This "vee" in the feminine form represents the womb of Mary Magdalene who was (supposedly) married to Jesus Christ and the union produced a daughter which began a Royal Bloodline. When the Holy Grail legend speaks of "the chalice that held the blood of Christ", it actually refers to Mary Magdalene—the female womb that carried the Jesus Royal Bloodline and created a new birth.

And now for the interesting part. The original icon for a male in this same historical time was the *inverted vee* as shown below:

Apparently, the symbol for the masculine "chalice" was incorrectly (intentionally) reversed and converted or made into a feminine "chalice" according to Brown's book. This was very clever, but not historically accurate.

The Response

If there ever were a counterfeit, this would be the real thing. A cleverly constructed counterfeit will have some aspects that appear to be real, but upon closer inspection and analysis we find that, although there are some truths woven throughout the book's fabric, those truths are drowned out by the not so subtle fabrications. In the search for truth, the bottom line is if it is not the whole truth, it is therefore a lie and nothing more than an entertaining story.

Consider this: as a male "chalice", the inverted vee would represent the person Jesus Christ and his spilled blood, which allows us to obtain a spiritual new birth into heaven. This then would be the real "Holy Grail" that many people have been in search of their entire lives.

Thus, this book—The Da Vinci Code—takes the real fact or truth and cleverly re-creates it as the opposite scenario in a master deception using similar facts, and taking ordinary meanings of words and phrases out of context in order to accomplish the desired result. The result is that the book has created a false religious belief that is today negatively affecting the spiritual lives of many people around the world.

The Scientific Evidence

In the graph and chart below, we demonstrate with scientific evidence that the book, The Da Vinci Code, does not conform to the Law of First Digits and therefore does not represent the entire truth.

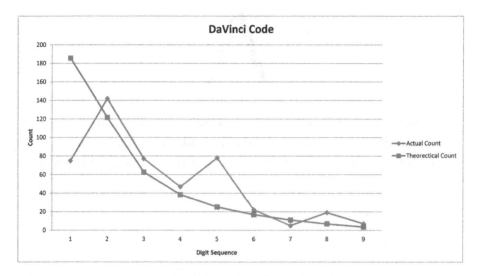

IMPORTED TEST DATA			First Digit	First Order	$\ddot{X}$	X	X - $\ddot{X}$	X - $\ddot{X}$	ESD	(Z)	(Z)^2
DaVinci Code					Theorectical Proportion	Theorectical Popiulation	Actual Popiulation	2 decimals	Rounded		$\dfrac{X - \ddot{X}}{ESD}$	
Digit	Count	% of Total									
1	75	15.89%	1		0.3932	186	75	-110.59	-111.00	9.97	-11.14	124.07
2	142	30.08%	2		0.2576	122	142	20.41	20.00	8.28	2.42	5.84
3	77	16.31%	3		0.1327	63	77	14.37	14.00	7.18	1.95	3.80
4	47	9.96%	4		0.0815	38	47	8.53	9.00	6.43	1.40	1.96
5	78	16.53%	5		0.0534	25	78	52.80	53.00	5.87	9.04	81.64
6	22	4.66%	6		0.0358	17	22	5.10	5.00	5.43	0.92	0.85
7	5	1.06%	7		0.0235	11	5	-6.09	-6.00	5.08	-1.18	1.40
8	19	4.03%	8		0.0146	7	19	12.11	12.00	4.79	2.51	6.28
9	7	1.48%	9		0.0077	4	7	3.37	3.00	4.54	0.66	0.44
	472		Totals		1.0000	472	472				$\sum (Z)^2 =$	226.26

Chi- Square		214.4575303
Conformity is anything <8		

	ESD Estimated Standard Deviation			
First Digit		ACTUAL		
	CONSTANT	POPULATION	SUM	SQ RT
1	0.2104	472	99.31	9.97
2	0.1451	472	68.49	8.28
3	0.1093	472	51.59	7.18
4	0.0875	472	41.30	6.43
5	0.0729	472	34.41	5.87
6	0.0625	472	29.50	5.43
7	0.0546	472	25.77	5.08
8	0.0486	472	22.94	4.79
9	0.0437	472	20.63	4.54

With a Chi Square score of 214.46, it is clear, as with the analysis of other documents, that this book is _un_natural and therefore false in its contention that the feminine vee (**V**) is the symbol of the "Holy Grail" that was embodied in the person of Mary. It does, however, strongly support our contention that the *male icon of the inverted vee* (Λ) *is the correct symbol of the "Holy Grail" that the world has been searching for through many centuries without any meaningful results.* Is it possible that the true "Holy Grail" can now be found and identified!

Origin of the Species

Since our first book, *The Organized Universe,* took dead aim at Darwinian evolution and scientifically disproved its major thesis of natural selection and thereby invalidating the entire theory, it would only be appropriate to analyze Darwin's original book, which literally changed the world of science and established a lasting negative impact on theology.

In 1859, The Origin of Species by Charles Darwin burst upon the public conscience, forever altering man's psyche in understanding from whence he came. Darwin's Evolutionary Theory was in actuality a number of theories, the five (5) most prominent of which were finally accepted by biologists over the succeeding 80+ years after the publication and the two closest competing theories faded away after only 40 years. His theory is more correctly called "the theory of evolution by natural selection". Evolution, after all, is just change. Darwin's proposal was that random mutations occur between generations, and that some of these mutations through their offspring are more useful than others in helping individuals survive their environments. Furthermore, that the lineages of living things change, diverge and go extinct over time, rather than appear suddenly in immutable form. Those who survive reproduce and so pass on these helpful traits to their off—spring. Another way to state it is that all life and eventually man himself simply evolved from lifeless matter over billions of years through countless iterations of mutations involving a process known as 'natural selection'. Either way, it was implied that man descended from the apes and that is what caused the firestorm to this day. There have been numerous publications espousing the pros and cons of evolution over the years with all the serious criticisms having been refuted or ignored. In our first groundbreaking book, *The Organized Universe,* we demonstrated scientifically using the Law of First Digits that the mechanism of natural selection cannot operate in an ordered universe but only in a chaotic array or disorder of matter. It can be categorically stated that *The Organized Universe* cannot be refuted as it is scientifically sound and it certainly cannot be ignored.

Since this book is the basis for Darwinism and the subject of so much controversy, we decided to apply the Law of First Digits to see, in this alternate way, if it conforms to the law and is therefore true or not. Again, as you can clearly see from the chart and graph below it does not conform, and with a high Chi Square score of 154 it is far from the truth. (Remember, a score of <8 denotes a perfect to better than perfect fit.) Even the lynch pin of godless atheism wrapped in secular naturalism cannot stand up to true scientific scrutiny. Again, you can draw your own conclusions.

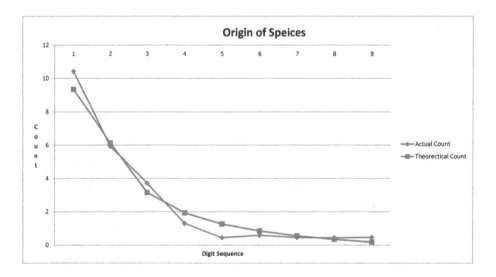

Futher Analysis on Books

IMPORTED TEST DATA			First Digit	First Order	$\bar{X}$	X	X - $\bar{X}$	X - $\bar{X}$	ESD	(Z)	(Z)²
Origin of Species					Theorectical Proportion	Theorectical Population	Actual Poplulation	2 decimals	Rounded	$\dfrac{X - \bar{X}}{ESD}$	
Digit	Count	% of Total									
1	1042	43.82%	1		0.3932	935	1042	106.97	107.00	22.37	4.78	22.88
2	592	24.89%	2		0.2576	613	592	-20.57	-21.00	18.58	-1.13	1.28
3	372	15.64%	3		0.1327	316	372	56.44	56.00	16.12	3.47	12.07
4	131	5.51%	4		0.0815	194	131	-62.81	-63.00	14.42	-4.37	19.07
5	45	1.89%	5		0.0534	127	45	-81.99	-82.00	13.17	-6.23	38.79
6	59	2.48%	6		0.0358	85	59	-26.13	-26.00	12.19	-2.13	4.55
7	46	1.93%	7		0.0235	56	46	-9.88	-10.00	11.39	-0.88	0.77
8	44	1.85%	8		0.0146	35	44	9.28	9.00	10.75	0.84	0.70
9	47	1.98%	9		0.0077	18	47	28.69	29.00	10.19	2.84	8.09
	2378		Totals		1.0000	2378	2378				Σ(Z)² =	108.20

need to import directly from program

Chi- Square	154.3252405

Conformity is anything <8

	E S D Estimated Standard Deviation			
First Digit	CONSTANT	ACTUAL POPULATION	SUM	SQ RT
1	0.2104	2378	500.33	22.37
2	0.1451	2378	345.05	18.58
3	0.1093	2378	259.92	16.12
4	0.0875	2378	208.08	14.42
5	0.0729	2378	173.36	13.17
6	0.0625	2378	148.63	12.19
7	0.0546	2378	129.84	11.39
8	0.0486	2378	115.57	10.75
9	0.0437	2378	103.92	10.19

Of course there are thousands of other books and documents that could be analyzed but this initial sampling should give you a good idea of where the tests are headed as to what conforms to the law and what doesn't. So far, only the Holy Bible has met this very ridged test; however, this does not mean that other books and documents will be found to conform and with independent verification. Our cutting edge research into natural truth of things will be an ongoing project and, when completed, the results will be documented in a new book.

CHAPTER 7

The Other Language of the Bible

First, let us explore a little history of the Bible and inquire about what languages are contained in the Bible?

Pastors, scholars and seminarians can answer this question easily, but the general populace may have only a vague idea that the Bible was written in one of those "dead" languages of ancient Greek or Latin.

What we will discover is that the Bible was actually written in three different ancient languages: Hebrew, Aramaic, and Greek. Although true that modern versions of these languages are spoken today, these modern readers would have some difficulty with the ancient version used in the Biblical texts. Hardly anyone would recognize the most influential book in the world in its original form.

The first human author to write down the biblical record was Moses. He was commanded by God to take on this task, for Exodus 34:27 records God's words to Moses, "Write down these words, for in accordance with these words I have made a covenant with you and with Israel." And what language did he use? He wrote in his native language, called Hebrew.

Hebrew is one of a group of languages known as the Semitic languages dating back past 1500 BC. It was spoken throughout that part of the world, and then called Mesopotamia, located today mainly in Iraq. It was the tongue of the ancient Israelites and the language in which most of the Old Testament is penned. Isaiah 19:8 calls it "the language of Canaan," while other verses label it "Judean" and "language of the Jews" (2 Kings 18:26; Isaiah 36:11, 13; 2 Chronicles 32:18; Nehemiah 13:24).[59]

The ancient Hebrew alphabet consisted of 22 letters, all of which were consonants and is written from right to left. (Imagine having an alphabet with no vowels? Much later, however, they did add the vowels.)

Almost the entire Old Testament was written in Hebrew during the thousand years of its composition. However, a few chapters in the prophecies of Ezra and Daniel and one verse in Jeremiah were written in a language called Aramaic. This language became very popular in the ancient world and actually displaced many other languages. Aramaic even became the common language spoken in Israel in Jesus' time, and was likely the language He spoke day by day. Some Aramaic words were even used by the Gospel writers in the New Testament.

The New Testament, however, was written in Greek. This seems strange, since you might think it would be either Hebrew or Aramaic. By the time the Gospels were being written, many Jews did not even speak Hebrew anymore. Rome had conquered Greece and the influence of Greek culture was still pervasive throughout the empire. However, Greek was the language of scholarship during the years of the composition of the New Testament from 50 to 100 AD by most accounts. The fact that many Jews could not even speak or read Hebrew anymore greatly disturbed the Jewish leaders. Therefore, around 300 BC a translation of the Old Testament from Hebrew into Greek was undertaken and completed around 200 BC. Gradually, this Greek translation of the Old Testament, called the Septuagint, was widely accepted and was even used in many synagogues. It also became a wonderful missionary tool for the early Christians, for now the Greeks could read God's Word in their own tongue.

So, the New Testament authors wrote in Greek. However, they did not use really high-class or classical Greek, but a very common and everyday type of Greek called *koine* or common Greek which could be easily understood by almost anyone, educated or not. For many years, some scholars ridiculed the Greek of the New Testament because many of its words were strange to those who read the writings of the great Greek classical authors such as Plato and Aristotle. Nevertheless, many records were later uncovered of ordinary people, and amazingly, they found the same common terms used in everyday speech. The ridicule dried up accordingly.

The earliest copies of parts of the Hebrew Old Testament were discovered in 1947. They are part of the famous Dead Sea Scrolls and actually date back to the first century BC. Even though they are at least 900 years older than any parts of the Bible we had before this, they are not the originals. They are copies. The originals have all been lost or destroyed. However, we are not at all doubtful that we may not have the original text. Copying by scribes was done with great care in those days and because the text was regarded as sacred, the copyists were extremely painstaking. Today some 5000 hand copied documents exist of all or part of the Bible, and they agree in 98% of the text! No other ancient writing has this amount of underlying support with such amazing agreement as to the text.

Yes, we do have what God wanted us to have! By way of translation, we now have His revelation in our own language and in 2300 other languages, too. Today we have the very Bible that comes to us from the three languages used in the original. Truly, we can say, "God speaks my language, too!" [60]

The Fourth Language of the Bible

But wait. God speaks to us in yet another way, another language. It is the Fourth Language of the Bible – that of *mathematics*. We found in Chapter 4 that there were 3,013 natural numbers [one (1) through nine (9)] contained in the Bible and that these numbers speak certain understandings involving the truth and trustworthiness of Holy Scripture based on their conformity to the Law of First Digits or Benford's Law. In connecting all the dots, we can begin to see new relationships that form what we call the Three Strands of Truth:

1. **Benford's Law of First Digits** – a proven natural law of science revealing consistent, yet skewed logarithmic distributions or patterns revealing true physical arrangements of elemental composition of matter proving a universal order. The law also measures conformity and non-conformity to true life happenings, occurrences and events here on earth. We sometimes call Benford's Law, the Law of Laws since it is one of God's physical laws of

the universe and is embedded in all the fundamental physical constants or laws of the universe.

2. **Hand Book of Chemistry & Physics, 88ᵗʰ Edition,** published by the National Institute of Standards and Technology provides a broad coverage of all types of physical science data commonly encountered by scientists and engineers. It also describes the fundamental physical constants known in the universe and how they are constant and invariant over time.

3. **Old & New Testaments (KJV)** – the Holy Scripture that contains the language of mathematics making the invisible visible through the Law of First Digits.

Now, we have learned that the Bible consists of four languages, with the fourth one confirming the validity of the other three. In summary then, we have the following:

1. Ancient Hebrew (majority of the Old Testament, later translated in Greek and called the Septuagint)
2. Aramaic (a small percentage of the Old Testament, but became the common day language of Jesus' time)
3. Greek (the majority of the New Testament as translated from the ancient Hebrew)
4. Mathematics (the hidden order of God's symmetry in both nature and His Holy Word)

Therefore, we can conclude that if mathematics is one of the languages of the Bible and is represented by a natural law of science (the Law of First Digits); and we know that all natural laws of science are invariant, we then have the following logical deduction:

1. If the fundamental physical constants of the universe as used in the equations of physics describing these laws are themselves invariant,
2. And if the Law of First Digits is proven to be a true natural law of science and itself is invariant,
3. And to which all the natural laws conform,

4. And if the Word of God as revealed in the Bible (the King James Version as well as in the original Hebrew, Aramaic and Greek) conforms to Benford's Law of First Digits, (one of His laws)

5. Then the only logical conclusion is that the Bible is proven by one of God's own natural laws and is, in fact, invariant and inerrant, thus revealing the True God of the Universe and His authentic Word.

We are hopeful that the proof presented here will (1) serve as a "truth buffer" to help level the playing field and eliminate the endless wrangling and controversies inherent among all religion, and (2) to establish a common benchmark from which all of us can discern the truth using a basic application of one of the true natural laws of science.

Relative to the subject of this book, the question should not be "who is right or who is wrong?" but, more rationally, "is my religious faith based on a truth and can that truth be proven scientifically?"

Today, most Christians employ a "leap of faith" in their approach to God, His Holy Word, and the articles of Christian faith, particularly with plans and methods that they do not understand. But this leap of faith need not be a blind one. As John Clayton says in The Source, "…God does not require such a mindless commitment but rather asks us to leap *based upon rational, understandable evidence that he has provided in abundance*".[61] Emphasis added.

To deny God, a person must ignore a great deal of not just favorable evidence but scientific evidence as we have shown throughout this book. The personal and social consequences of such a denial should be obvious. We trust that the arguments in this book will help you make your own "leap of faith" based on rational, understandable evidence outside of the Scriptures themselves.

The Path to Salvation: Connecting the Dots from Reality to Salvation

The old Latin proverb, *Veritas vos liberabit* meaning the truth shall set you free, was never truer than when applied to the revealed truths of the Bible. For once we have determined that the Bible is in fact the true inspired Word of God, and that the Christian Faith is a realistic faith based on our ability to use our natural senses,[62] we realize there is direct connection between reality and salvation.

Without becoming too philosophical, trying to define reality is a bit like trying to define everyone else's "perception of reality" using a one-size-fits-all sentence containing only one verb, one adjective and one article. Obviously, that is impossible. Others will say reality is language or consciousness or things that are observable and comprehensible—all of which would not exist without some form of reality. And on it goes in a never ending cacophony of philosophical vagueness and idealism.

However, another more practical view (one to which we ascribe) is that reality is what actually exist and is most fundamental in the universe. In order to find out why things (that we know exist) behave the way they do, you have to go below the surface to find that everything is made of molecules and molecules are just clusters of atoms and they in turn are just groups of protons, neutrons and electrons; and on it goes into quarks and leptons then into that mysterious "something" that holds it all together. Don't worry, we are not delving into string theory here, but suffice it to say that all these microscopic particles of matter just discussed occupy what is called "space-time" which is defined by coordinates (i.e., x, y, z for space and t for time at least in the third dimension) which are nothing more than numbers. Numbers are what constitute the basis of our reality. Although numbers are just a concept to each of us, they are nonetheless the same everybody. The number 5 to me is the same as the number 5 to you and anyone else in the world who understands the basic number system. Therefore, the most fundamental thing that exists and forms the basis for everything else is math. Everything from matter to the abstractness of consciousness (i.e., from perception to brain to biology to chemistry to physics) can be reduced down to math.

Having said all of the above, here is a list of how the dots are connected:

1. Everyone should have the same sense of reality.
2. And that we understand and observe this reality through our natural senses.
3. And all will agree that we live in a world and universe consisting of natural laws of science and certain logic principles which are proven true through the use of the Scientific Method.

4. Now the results of this scientific method can be observed and verified with the logic of a clear mind by using our natural senses.

5. One of these true natural laws of science that can be observed and verified is known as the Law of First Digits or Benford's law, which measures the true arrangement of matter and other things.

6. Through observable testing and verification, we discover that the Holy Scriptures (both the Old and New Testaments) fit the exacting parameters of this newly discovered natural law of science.

7. Consequently, as we demonstrate in our two recent books, (*The Organized Universe* and *The DNA of Scripture: Bridging the Gap between Science, Intelligent Design and Religion*), the Holy Scriptures are logically true as a result of their conformity to this law.

8. As a result of this singular truth, the identity of the one true God and His true Son, Jesus Christ of Nazareth the Messiah, are revealed in the Holy Scriptures.

9. To further extend the logic of this truth, we notice that this same Holy Scripture teaches that righteousness and salvation come from reality and belief in the Resurrection of that same Messiah.

10. The Scriptures verify the Resurrection through a true record of natural senses, a scientific experiment and the logic of a clear mind.

11. Therefore, if this is reality, then the true reality is the true understanding of reality through true faith and belief that results in salvation.[63]

It is important to understand that the above description of the true pathway to faith and belief does not depend on any religious dogma, doctrine, blind faith or endless arguments of same. This is the only pathway that promotes true unity and love for one another.

Notes Regarding Logic Principles

Notwithstanding the vagaries of the psychology of reasoning (i.e., why some people do not reason correctly), let us stipulate that logic is, briefly speaking, defined as the study of the principles of *correct reasoning*. Therefore, the following general logic sequence applies:

- Eliminating fraud and trickery, what you observe with your natural senses is generally true.
- Eliminating fraud and trickery, what is proven by the Scientific Method is generally true.
- Again, eliminating fraud and trickery, therefore, if A = B and B = C, then A = C is generally true.

It is therefore the use of clear mind, simple logic and one of God's universal natural laws that we are able to identify the true God of the universe as revealed in His Holy Word.

With a subject as intricate and controversial as the Bible, we are sure that many questions will arise in the reader. With that in mind, we cordially invite you to write to us at the contact address below and submit your questions. We are most happy to clarify any information, theories or ideas we have given you in the hope that your perception may be changed or enhanced in a positive way regarding your new-found view of the Bible.

Karl L. Dahlstrom
2591 Dallas Parkway
Suite 107
Frisco, TX 75034

I will leave you with these parting words from Romans 1:19-20:
"For that which is known about God is evident to them and made plain in their inner consciousness, because God [Himself] has shown it to them.

For even since the creation of the world His invisible nature and attributes, this, His eternal power and divinity, have been made intelligible and clearly discernable in and through the things that have been made (His handiworks). So [men] are without excuse [altogether without any defense or justification]." **AMPV**

APPENDIXES

1. **Miscellaneous Quote:** In discussing how and when God intervened in his progressive creation to produce the complex web of life we observe all around us, quantum chemist and five-time nominee for the Noble prize, Henrey F. Schaefer mused, "The significance and joy in my science comes in those occasional moments of discovering something new and say to myself, 'So that's how God did it.' My goal is to understand a little corner of god's plan" (Sheler and Schrof 1991, 7).

2. **A Short Synopsis of The Organized Universe:** In *The Organized Universe*, we painstakingly demonstrated the applicability and conformity of the Law of First Digits to a broad sampling of the natural world. This sampling includes the composition of seawater, the earth's crust, mammalian cells, solar system satellites of the planets, internal structure of the sun, physical features of gulfs and bays, US county population counts, musical scales and many more. (Since the publishing of The Organized Universe, scientists have discovered even more examples of the conformity of Benford to the natural world. Here we proved the underlying law of order in the universe and its interrelationship to the fundamental physical constants that regulate our world. This proof was intentionally accomplished without reference to God, a Supreme Being, Creator or Designer of the Universe for the following two reasons:

   a. To utilize the scientific method to disprove Darwin's Theory of Evolution by attacking one of its primary postulates, that of Natural Selection. In doing so, we demonstrated through the use of Benford's Law of First Digits that all matter was and is an ordered array or pattern and not that of chaos and disorder as mandated by evolutionary theory.

b. To circumvent the prohibition contained in the Establishment Clause of the First Amendment to the Constitution in the use of any religious reference or theory in the teaching of any life sciences with regard to origin and development of life on earth.

3. Sample of the Author's original tally sheets when counting significant digits in the Bible.

5 And a tenth part of an ephah of flour for a meat offering, mingled with the fourth part of an hin of beaten oil.

6 It is a continual burnt offering, which was ordained in mount Sinai for a sweet savour, a sacrifice made by fire unto the LORD.

7 And the drink offering thereof shall be the fourth part of an hin for the one lamb: in the holy place shalt thou cause the strong wine to be poured unto the LORD for a drink offering.

8 And the other lamb shalt thou offer at even: as the meat offering of the morning, and as the drink offering thereof, thou shalt offer it, a sacrifice made by fire, of a sweet savour unto the LORD.

9 And on the sabbath day two lambs of the first year without spot, and two tenth deals of flour for a meat offering, mingled with oil, and the drink offering thereof:

10 This is the burnt offering of every sabbath, beside the continual burnt offering, and his drink offering.

11 And in the beginnings of your months ye shall offer a burnt offering unto the LORD; two young bullocks, and one ram, seven lambs of the first year without spot;

12 And three tenth deals of flour for a meat offering, mingled with oil, for one bullock; and two tenth deals of flour for a meat offering, mingled with oil, for one ram;

13 And a several tenth deal of flour mingled with oil for a meat offering unto one lamb; for a burnt offering of a sweet savour, a sacrifice made by fire unto the LORD.

14 And their drink offerings shall be half an hin of wine unto a bullock, and the third part of an hin unto a ram, and a fourth part of an hin unto a lamb: this is the burnt offering of every month throughout the months of the year.

15 And one kid of the goats for a sin offering unto the LORD shall be offered, beside the continual burnt offering, and his drink offering.

16 And in the fourteenth day of the first month is the passover of the LORD.

17 And in the fifteenth day of this month is the feast: seven days shall unleavened bread be eaten.

18 In the first day shall be an holy convocation; ye shall do no manner of servile work therein:

19 But ye shall offer a sacrifice made by fire for a burnt offering unto the LORD; two young bullocks, and one ram, and seven lambs of the first year: they shall be unto you without blemish:

20 And their meat offering shall be of flour mingled with oil: three tenth deals shall ye offer for a bullock, and two tenth deals for a ram;

21 A several tenth deal shalt thou offer for every lamb, throughout the seven lambs:

22 And one goat for a sin offering, to make an atonement for you.

23 Ye shall offer these beside the burnt offering in the morning, which is for a continual burnt offering.

24 After this manner ye shall offer daily, throughout the seven days, the meat of the sacrifice made by fire, of a sweet savour unto the LORD: it shall be offered beside the continual burnt offering, and his drink offering.

25 And on the seventh day ye shall have an holy convocation; ye shall do no servile work.

26 Also in the day of the firstfruits, when ye bring a new meat offering unto the LORD, after your weeks be out, ye shall have an holy convocation; ye shall do no servile work:

27 But ye shall offer the burnt offering for a sweet savour unto the LORD; two young bullocks, one ram, seven lambs of the first year;

28 And their meat offering of flour mingled with oil, three tenth deals unto one bullock, two tenth deals unto one ram,

29 A several tenth deal unto one lamb, throughout the seven lambs;

30 And one kid of the goats, to make an atonement for you.

31 Ye shall offer them beside the continual burnt offering, and his meat offering, (they shall be unto you without blemish) and their drink offerings.

CHAPTER 29

AND in the seventh month, on the first day of the month, ye shall have an holy convocation; ye shall do no servile work: it is a day of blowing the trumpets unto you.

2 And ye shall offer a burnt offering for a sweet savour unto the LORD; one young bullock, one ram, and seven lambs of the first year without blemish:

3 And their meat offering mingled with oil, three ten ock, and two tenth deals f

4 And one tenth dea throughout the seven lamb

5 And one kid of the goat: to make an atonement for

6 Beside the burnt offer and his meat offering, anc offering, and his meat offeri offerings, according unto t a sweet savour, a sacrifice the LORD.

7 And ye shall have on this seventh month an holy ye shall afflict your souls: any work therein:

8 But ye shall offer a the LORD for a sweet sav bullock, one ram, and sev first year; they shall be u blemish:

9 And their meat offering mingled with oil, three tentl ock, and two tenth deals to

10 A several tenth dea throughout the seven lambs

11 One kid of the goats f beside the sin offering of the continual burnt offering offering of it, and their drink

12 And on the fifteenth da month ye shall have an ho ye shall do no servile worl keep a feast unto the LORD

13 And ye shall offer a b sacrifice made by fire, of a unto the LORD; thirteen day rams, and fourteen lambs o they shall be without blemisl

14 And their meat offering mingled with oil, three tenth d bullock of the thirteen bullo deals to each ram of the two

15 And a several tenth de: of the fourteen lambs:

16 And one kind of the offering; beside the continual his meat offering, and his dri

17 And on the second day twelve young bullocks, two i lambs of the first year withou

18 And their meat offering offerings for the bullocks, for

166

First Digit – First Order

Date 11-19-91

Initial _____

First Digit	Word Equivalent	Population	Population Totals-Digit
1	O.T. – one, once	682	
	N.T. – one	296	978
2	O.T. – two, twain, twice, two edged, both, double	602	
	N.T. – two, twain, twice, two-edged, twofold, both, double	153	755
3	O.T. – three, threefold, thrice	293	
	N.T. – three, thrice	81	374
4	O.T. – four, fourfold	163	
	N.T. – four, fourfold, four footed	37	200
5	O.T. – five	152	
	N.T. – five	35	187
6	O.T. – six	93	
	N.T. – six	11	104
7	O.T. – seven	280	
	N.T. – seven	89	369
8	O.T. – eight	28	
	N.T. – eight	5	33
9	O.T. – nine	12	
	N.T. – nine	1	13
	O.T + N.T. Totals →	3,013	3,013

O.T. Totals → 2,305
N.T. Totals → 708
O.T. + N.T. Total → 3,013

4. Summary of applications of the Law of First Digits

Summary of Applications of the Law of First Digits

No	Selected Parameter	Reference Source	Total Population	Maximum + Z	Maximum -Z	$\sum (z)2$	Chi Square
1	Fundamental Physical Constants	CRC Handbook	191	+1.42	-1.24	6.30	5.25
2	Fundamental Physical Constants	Am. J. Phys	20	1.79	-1.18	8.64	8.67
3	Elements in Earth's Crust	CRC Handbook	88	+0.97	-1.28	5.05	4.49
4	Elements in Earth's Sea	CRC Handbook	81	+0.58	-1.06	1.85	1.66
5	V.D.W. Constants for Gas	CRC Handbook	86	+0.47	-0.46	1.09	0.95
6	Satellite Distances from Planets	CRC Handbook	61	+1.54	-1.23	11.41	9.89
7	Luminosities for Stars	Britannica	28	+0.81	-0.50	1.08	0.83
8	Temperatures within the Sun	Britannica	12	+1.15	-1.39	6.51	4.50
9	Maximum Depths of gulfs and Bays	Britannica	26	+1.45	-0.93	7.35	6.99
10	Gamma Transition Rates	Britannica	10	+1.18	-1.43	5.25	3.00
11	Coal Geologic Resources	Britannica	12	+0.76	-1.39	3.86	2.50
12	Areas of Oceans & Seas	Time Almanac	18	+1.89	-1.12	7.39	7.53
13	Acreage of National Historical Parks	Time Almanac	39	+1.05	-1.18	4.19	3.61
14	Percent Protein in Animal Feeds	Britannica	40	+0.54	-0.74	1.86	1.66
15	Percent Fiber in Animal Feeds	Britannica	34	+1.87	-1.37	7.75	7.00
16	Composition of Mammalian Cell	Britannica	8	+2.38	-1.30	9.88	8.58
17	National Consensus (1790–2000)	Time Almanac	22	+1.02	-1.44	5.19	5.25
18	Deaths from Volcanic Eruptions	Time Almanac	24	+0.98	-1.64	5.37	4.89
19	Drainage Discharge of World Rivers (1)	Britannica	27	+2.14	-1.30	11.46	10.46
20	Drainage Discharge of World Rivers (2)	Britannica	27	+1.75	-0.92	7.08	7.53
21	Drainage Discharge of World Rivers (3)	Britannica	27	+0.88	-1.43	4.71	4.53
22	Frequencies of Musical Scales	CRC Handbook	97	+1.07	-0.87	3.57	3.09
23	Influence of Pressure on Liquids	CRC Handbook	52	+1.89	-1.68	11.98	11.55
24	Diffusion Coefficients in Liquids	CRC Handbook	118	+1.67	-2.76	17.44	
25	U.S. County Populations 1930	Proceedings of American Philosophical Society	3259	+4.73	-6.45	133.51	
26	U.S. County Populations 1990	Benford's Law – Nigrini	3141	+1.79	-2.59	17.03	
27	Average Budget for an American Home	U.S. Bureau of Labor Statistics	15	+1.10	-1.23	5.64	
28	Earth Crust Elements - % Volume	Contemporary GEO	8	+4.17	-1.87	21.41	

5. Instructions for Statistical Analysis of the Law of First Digits are found below including Blank Forms for your own Analysis.

The Formulas used for Standard Deviation—Z Score and Chi-Square—along with the charts that should assist in the calculations are found on the following pages. The reader is encouraged to use these formulas and charts to verify the calculation number results in this book as well as to apply them to other measurements of the Universe and Planet Earth. We would appreciate your sharing your results with us.

The Statistical Mathematics Involved

The Calculations:

Starting with a certain total population of measurements or numbers that have resulted from true real life happenings and events or true physical arrangements of nature, the first digits 1 through 9 are tallied and then independently counted for each of the first digits 1 through 9 derived from those numbers.

First, a ratio of the independent count for each first digit is made with the total population of numbers used for the first digits 1 through 9. For example, if the count for the first digit one (1) is X, and the Total Population for the first digits 1 through 9 is N, the ratio would be:

Ratio= X_1/N; if $X_1 = 14$ and N=45, then

Ratio =14/45

and the decimal proportion is derived by dividing 45 into 14 which equals .3111- to four (4) decimal places.

Likewise, if first digit nine (9) X_9, is 2 and N=45, then Ratio= X_9 = 2/45 = .0444

The decimal proportion .3111 can be changed into a percentage by multiplying it by 100 or moving the decimal point two (2) places to the right.

Therefore, .3111 becomes 31.11% (Percent)

and

.0444 becomes 4.44% (Percent)

Next, the (Z) score or the number of standard deviations from the theoretical count $\bar{X}$ needs to be determined for each first digit 1 - 9.

167

First, a theoretical count $\ddot{X}$ needs to be calculated and determined. If the theoretical proportion **P** for the first digit 1 is .3010, then by multiplying that theoretical proportion of .3010 by the Total Population N of all the First Digits 1–9 we get 45. This is the theoretical count $\ddot{X}$. The Theoretical property P is obtained from the table of proportions for the Law of First Digits.

$$\ddot{X}_1 = P1 \times N \text{ or,}$$

$$\ddot{X}_1 = .3010 \times 45 = 13.55 \text{ or } 14 \text{ (rounded up)}$$

Then the difference or deviation with the Actual Count X can be determined which is:

$$X_1 - \ddot{X}_1; \text{ if } X_1 = 10 \text{ and } \ddot{X}_1 = 14, \text{ then } X_1 - \ddot{X}_1 = -4$$

The number of Standard Deviations or the (Z) score of a deviation of $X - \ddot{X}$ is calculated by:

(Z) score = $\underline{X - \ddot{X}}$;   where ESD is the Estimated Standard Deviation which is derived from the following formula where:

$$ESD = \sqrt{[(1-P) \times P] \times N} \quad ESD = \sqrt{[(1-P) \times P] \times P}$$

Where

P-Theoretical Proportion
N-Total Population of First Digits 1 – 9; If P=.3010 and

N=45 then,

$$ESD_1 = \sqrt{[(1-.3010) \times .3010] \times 45}$$

$$ESD_1 = \sqrt{.2104 \times 45} \qquad = \sqrt{9.47} \qquad = 3.08$$

Again, (Z_1) Score $= \dfrac{X_1 - \ddot{X}_1}{ESD_1}$

Or

$X_1 - \ddot{X}_1 = -4$ and $ESD_1 = 3.08$

Therefore,

(Z_1) Score $= \dfrac{-4}{3.08} = 1.30$ Standard Deviations from the theoretical count $\ddot{X}_1$

Each of the other First Digits Actual Counts of X is treated in the same manner.

To test how good a fit the Actual Count X_1 is in comparison to the Theoretical Count $\ddot{X}_1$ taking into consideration the Total Population of all of the First Digits 1- 9 which is 45, the application of the Chi-Square (pronounced "keigh square) formulas to the (Z) score is considered to be a very severe test even for large populations.

In analyzing the Chi-Squire formula, we add everything together or sum up everything using the symbol $\sum$.

So, Chi-square=

$$\sum (Z)^2 \text{ or } \sum [(Z_1)^2 + (Z_2)^2 + \ldots\ldots(Z_9)^2]$$

Each (z) score is squared and then added together or summed up.

Another second type of Chi-Square test is accomplished by using the following

formula: Chi- Square test is accomplished by using the following formula:

$$\text{Chi-Square} = \sum_{1}^{9} \left[\dfrac{(X - \ddot{X})^2}{X}\right]$$

$$\text{Chi-Square} = \sum \left[\dfrac{(X_1 - \ddot{X}_1)^2}{\ddot{X}_1} + \dfrac{(X_2 - \ddot{X}_2)^2}{\ddot{X}_1} + \ldots\ldots\dfrac{(X_9 - \ddot{X}_9)^2}{\ddot{X}_1}\right]$$

Where:

X = Actual Count for each First Digit 1 thru 9

Ẍ = Theoretical Count for each First Digit 1 thru 9

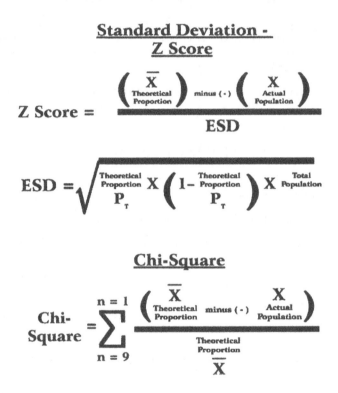

**Standard Deviation -
Z Score**

$$Z\ Score = \frac{\left(\overline{X}_{\substack{Theoretical \\ Proportion}}\right)\ minus\ (-)\ \left(X_{\substack{Actual \\ Population}}\right)}{ESD}$$

$$ESD = \sqrt{\underset{P_T}{\overset{Theoretical}{Proportion}} X \left(1 - \underset{P_T}{\overset{Theoretical}{Proportion}}\right) X \overset{Total}{Population}}$$

Chi-Square

$$Chi\text{-}Square = \sum_{n=9}^{n=1} \frac{\left(\overline{X}_{\substack{Theoretical \\ Proportion}}\ minus\ (-)\ X_{\substack{Actual \\ Population}}\right)}{\underset{\overline{X}}{\overset{Theoretical}{Proportion}}}$$

First Digit n	P_T Theoretical Proportion	$\overline{X}$ Theoretical Population	$\overline{X}$ Actual Population	$X - \overline{X}$	ESD	(Z) $\dfrac{X - \overline{X}}{ESD}$	P_A Actual Proportion
1							
2							
3							
4							
5							
6							
7							
8							
9							
Totals						$\sum(Z)^2 =$	
						chi - square	

$$ESD = \sqrt{P_T \ (1 - P_T) \ \text{x Total Population}}$$

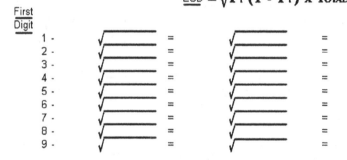

First
Digit
1 - √‾‾‾‾‾ =   √‾‾‾‾‾ =
2 - √‾‾‾‾‾ =   √‾‾‾‾‾ =
3 - √‾‾‾‾‾ =   √‾‾‾‾‾ =
4 - √‾‾‾‾‾ =   √‾‾‾‾‾ =
5 - √‾‾‾‾‾ =   √‾‾‾‾‾ =
6 - √‾‾‾‾‾ =   √‾‾‾‾‾ =
7 - √‾‾‾‾‾ =   √‾‾‾‾‾ =
8 - √‾‾‾‾‾ =   √‾‾‾‾‾ =
9 - √‾‾‾‾‾ =   √‾‾‾‾‾ =

6. The Symmetry of Scripture

The Symmetry of Scripture

Although English-speakers often think of the Bible as containing 66 books—39 in the Old Testament and 27 in the New Testament—the ancient Hebrew reckoning divided the Old Testament into 22 books. Therefore, we can see that the Bible consists of a canon of 49 books—seven times seven—a number used throughout Scripture to indicate completion. In turn, the 49 books can be classified into seven subdivisions.

Old Testament

I. The Law
The five "Books of Moses" begin with the creation, and continue through the giving of the Law and the early history of the Israelites.

1. Genesis
2. Exodus
3. Leviticus
4. Numbers
5. Deuteronomy

II. The Prophets
The next six books contain accounts of, and prophecies by, Hebrew prophets after Moses.

6. Joshua-Judges
7. Samuel-Kings
8. Isaiah
9. Jeremiah
10. Ezekiel
11. The Twelve Minor Prophets

III. The Writings
Along with stories, essays, songs and poems, the Writings include histories of God's people from the Babylonian exile through the building of the second temple.

12. Psalms
13. Proverbs

14. Job
15. Song of Solomon
16. Ruth
17. Lamentations
18. Ecclesiastes
19. Esther
20. Daniel
21. Ezra-Nehemiah
22. Chronicles

New Testament

IV. Christ Establishes His Church
The four gospels and Acts recount Jesus Christ's birth, ministry, death and resurrection, and describe the establishment and early spread of the New Testament Church.

23. Matthew
24. Mark
25. Luke
26. John
27. Acts

V. The General Epistles
Church leaders originally addressed these letters to the "general" Church membership, rather than to any one congregation or person.

28. James
29. 1 Peter

30. 2 Peter
31. 1 John
32. 2 John
33. 3 John
34. Jude

VI. The Pauline Epistles
The Apostle Paul wrote these letters to congregations or individuals whom he served.

35. Romans
36. 1 Corinthians
37. 2 Corinthians
38. Galatians
39. Ephesians
40. Philippians
41. Colossians
42. 1 Thessalonians
43. 2 Thessalonians
44. Hebrews
45. 1 Timothy
46. 2 Timothy
47. Titus
48. Philemon

VII. The Prophecies
The Apostle John composed this mysterious book so that Christians could understand Church history and end-time events.

49. Revelation

Some Bibles include additional Old Testament books known as "Apocrypha." These are non-canonical texts, which are not considered inspired and cannot be relied upon for doctrine, but may occasionally be useful to clarify points of history. They were composed after Malachi (the latest Old Testament book, the last of the twelve minor prophets), but before the New Testament. Some non-canonical texts written after Christ's resurrection are also called "Apocrypha"—these cannot be trusted for history or doctrine, and were in many cases written to promote agendas opposed to Jesus Christ's actual teachings.

END NOTES

1   William A. Dembski, Intelligent Design, Intervarsity Press, 1999, p. 207
2   Gleason L. Archer, Jr., A Survey of Old Testament Introduction, 1974, p. 15).
3   Kerby Anderson, <u>A Biblical Point of View on Intelligent Design</u>, Harvest House Publishers, Eugene, Oregon, page 120.
4   Dr. Jason Lisle, "God and Natural Law", Answers Magazine, August 28, 2006, www.answersingenesis.org
5   Anthropic comes from the Greek word for man, Anthropos.
6   This phrase is attributed to the creation astronomer Johannes Kepler
7   Robert Pirsig, "Lila: An Inquiry into Morals," 1991; "…when one person suffers from a delusion it is called insanity. When many people suffer from a delusion it is called religion."
8   Grant R. Jeffrey, <u>The Signature of God, Word Publishing, Nashville, TN, Paraphrased from examples shown in Chapter 6, p.127.</u>
9   John Clayton, <u>The Source</u>, Howard Publishing 2001, pp. 42—43
10 Ribonucleic acid (RNA) is a polymeric molecule. It is implicated in a varied sort of biological roles in coding, decoding, regulation, and expression of genes. DNA and RNA are nucleic acids, and, along with proteins and carbohydrates, constitute the three major macromolecules essential for all known forms of life.
11 C. S. Lewis, The Magician's Twin, Discovery Institute Press, 2012.
12 Grant R. Jeffrey, in his Special Foreword to Yacov Rambsel's book, Yeshua – The Name of Jesus Revealed in Code in the Old Testament: Toronto: Frontier Research, 1996
13 Grant R. Jeffrey, The Mysterious Bible Codes, Word Publishing, 1998.
14 Michael Drosnin, The Bible Code (New York: Simon and Schuster, 1997)
15 James Giggacher, *The Rule of One*
16 M. Samabridge, H. Tkalčić, and A. Jackson, *Geophysical Research Letters, Vol. 37, L22301*, doi:10.1029/2010GL044830, 2010
17 Christopher J. Rosetti, CFE, CPA, *Using Benford's Law to Detect Fraud*, 2003.

[18] Mark J. Nigrini, *Digital Analysis Tests and Statistics – Using Microsoft Access for Data Analysis and Interrogation, 2002.*

[19] Ibid, p. 7

[20] Ibid, p. 8.

[21] J Torres, S Fernández, A Gamero and A Sola, "How do numbers begin?", Eur. J Phys 28 (2007) L17—L25

[22] ibid

[23] Gödel's incompleteness theorems are among the most important results in modern logic. These discoveries revolutionized the understanding of mathematics and logic, and had dramatic implications for the philosophy of mathematics. There have also been attempts to apply them in other fields of philosophy, but the legitimacy of many such applications is much more controversial. Stanford Encyclopedia of Philosophy;

[24] Mark J. Nigrini, Benford's Law: Tests and Statistics for Auditors, 2000, page 21.

[25] Ibid

[26] Hill, T.: "Nobody knows how fast you can get to Benford's Law – how many numbers need to be in a list before the digits will show a Benford distribution?"

[27] Mark J. Nigrini, Benford's Law: Applications for Forensic Accounting, Auditing and Fraud Detection, 2012, page 20.

[28] New Scientist, 10 July 1999

[29] Eigen, Manfred, 1992, *Steps Toward Life,* Oxford: Oxford University Press, p.12.

[30] Allen Butler, The Origin and History of the Number System, August 15, 2005,

[31] A geological doctrine that changes in the earth's crust have in the past been brought about suddenly by physical forces operating in ways that cannot be observed today—compare uniformitarianism; Marion-Webster dictionary/online

[32] M. King Hubbert, Stanford University

[33] A good description and explanation of this primordial environment is found in *Origins of Existence* by Fred Adams, 2002

[34] Ibid, p. 170.

[35] Jack Challoner, The Elements –The New Guide to Building Blocks of Our Universe, 2012, Table of Contents

[36] Ibid, page 153.

[37] CRC Handbook of Chemistry and Physics – 88th Edition; CRC Press 2007-2008, pages 14-17.

[38] Stan Gibilisco, Statistics Demystified, 2004, pages 119-120. "Sometimes you'll hear people say that such –and-such an observation or result is 23.2 standard deviations below the mean' or '1.6 standard deviations above the mean.' The *Z score,* symbolized z, is a quantitative measure of the position of a particular element with respect to the mean. The Z score of an element is equal to the

number of standard deviations that the element differs from the mean, either positively or negatively."

39 Murray R. Spiegel, <u>Schaums Outline Series – Theory and Problems of Statistics, Pages 201—202.</u> The Chi—Square (pronounced Keigh-Square) Test of-goodness-of-fit is "a measure of the discrepancy existing between observed and expected frequencies."

40 Statistically speaking means allowing for deviation from the mean and a small population

41 CRC Handbook, pages 14-17

42 "Practically speaking" means within a reasonably relevant and relative period of time.

43 CRC Handbook, Pages, 14-17.

44 Srinivasa Ramanujan FRS was an Indian mathematician and autodidact who, with almost no formal training in pure mathematics, made extraordinary contributions to mathematical analysis, number theory, infinite series, and continued fractions. www.Britanica.com

45 CRC Handbook, page 6-36.

46 CRC Handbook, page 1-1.

47 John Burke and Eric Kincanon, *Benford's law and physical constants: the distribution of initial digits,* American Journal of Physics, Vol. 59, No. 10, October 1991

48 P. Davies, *The Superforce: A Search for a Grand Unified Theory of Nature* (New York, Simon & Schuster, 1984, page 243.

49 Barnes' Notes on the Bible http://biblehub.com/commentaries/isaiah/42-9.htm

50 Dembski, *Intelligent Design,* pg. 17.

51 ibid

52 1_Comparison of Matthew thus John Plus Revelation
    2_MatthewThruActsPlusRevelation
    3_MatthewThruActsPlusRevelationAdjusted
    4_No.of FirstDigitsperO.T. and N.T. for Digit 1
    5_No.of FirstDigitsperO.T. and N.T. for Digit 2
    6_No.of FirstDigitsperO.T. and N.T. for Digit 3
    7_No.of FirstDigitsperO.T. and N.T. for Digit 4
    8_No.of FirstDigitsperO.T. and N.T. for Digit 5
    9_No.of FirstDigitsperO.T. and N.T. for Digit 6
    10_No.of FirstDigitsperO.T. and N.T. for Digit 7
    11_No.of FirstDigitsperO.T. and N.T. for Digit 8
    12_No.of FirstDigitsperO.T. and N.T. for Digit 9
    13_No.of FirstDigitsperO.T. and N.T. for Digit 1 thru 9
    14_SummationofFirstDigits1thru9
    15_BookofMormon

16_DoctrineandCovenants

17_NumNatNumperBookO.T.

18_NumNatNumperBookN.T.

19_NumChapperBookOldTes

20_NumChapperBookNewTes

21_NumVersesinOldTes

22_NumVersesinNewTes

23_OldTesNumWordsperBookO.T.

24_NewTesNumWordsperBookN.T.

25_OldTesNumLetperBookinO.T.

26_NewTesNumLetperBookinN.T.

27_SumOfNo.Nat.Num.Chap.Ver.WordsLetofO.T.N.T.

28_No.TimesWordFatherGodinGreekandEnglishperN.T.

29_No.TimesWordJesusisUsed per Book N.T.

30_No.TimesWordJesusisUsed per Book N.T.English

31_No.TimesWordHolySpiritinGreekEnglishinN.T.

32_No.TimesWordHolyGhostinGreekEnglishinN.T.

33_No.TimesWordHolyGhosandSpirtitinGreekEnglishinN.T.

34_No.TimesWordComFatherJesusSpiritGhost

35_No.TimesWordComFatherJesusSpiritGhostWordcount

36_No.TimesWordSaviorinGreekperN.T.

37_No.TimesWordSaviorinGreekperN.T.

38_No.TimesWordCrossinGreekisUsedinN.T.

39_No.TimesWordGrace

40_The Perfect Fit

41_OldTestTotalHebrewLetFrequencies

42_OldTestPerHebrewLetFreq

43_N.T.ScriptureCardinalNumbers(First Order)

44_No.TimestheWordFathersGod

45_Com.MatthewthruJohnplusRevelation

46_MatthewthruActsplusRevelation

47_Nat.CensusesU.S.ResidentPopulations

48_U.S.CountyPopCountsfor1990Census

49_InfluPressureFreezingPoints

53 The Pear of Great Price, Introduction, https://www.lds.org/scriptures/pgp/introduction?lang=eng

54 Steve Rudd, www.bible.ca/catholic-apocrypha.htm

55 www.gotquestions.org

56 Raymond Hammer, *The Eternal Teaching: Hinduism*, from Eerdmann's Handbook to the World's Religions, 1994,William B. Eerdmans Publishing Company, Grand Rapids, Michigan, p. 170.

[57] Secrets of the Code, 2004, Bernsteinp. xxv ii

[58] Cracking the Code, 2004, Garlow & Jones, p. 72

[59] http://www.biblegateway.com/blog/2012/06/What was the original language of the Bible/

[60] http://www.biblica.com/bibles/faq/11/

[61] John Clayton and Nils Jansma, 2001, The Source; Howard Publishing Company, West Monroe, La. Pg. 216.

[62] Karl L. Dahlstrom with C. Phillip Clegg, The 2nd Reformation, 2013, Outskirts Press, Inc.; for a full discussion of this subject see Chapter 2.

[63] The connection between item #5 and item #6 provides the nexus for the connection of the dots between items #1 thru #11 — this being Reality connected with Salvation. The True Natural Law of Science, item #5, when applied to the Holy Scripture, item #6, connects the gap between Reality and Salvation that has existed previously. This allows for a different and new pathway to a true faith in salvation